SKILLS FOR
Big Feelings

A Guide for Teaching Kids Relaxation, Regulation, and Coping Techniques

Written and illustrated by

Casey O'Brien Martin, LMHC, REAT, RN

Disclaimer

Names of people mentioned have been changed to protect the privacy of individuals. The information in this book is not intended or implied to be a substitute for professional medical advice, diagnosis, or treatment. Those responsible for the welfare of children should consult with professionals for matters relating to the child's health and particularly with respect to any symptoms that may require diagnosis or medical attention. If expert assistance or counseling is needed, the services of a competent professional should be sought.

Although every effort has been made to ensure that the information in this book is correct at the time of release, the author and publisher do not assume, and hereby disclaim, any liability to any party for any loss, damage, or disruption caused by errors or omissions of details, whether such errors or omissions result from negligence, accident, or any other cause.

Skills for Big Feelings A Guide for Teaching Kids Relaxation, Regulation, and Coping Techniques

Written and illustrated by Casey O'Brien Martin, LMHC, REAT, RN

Published by Whole Child Counseling

ISBN: 978-1-7355177-2-8

Table of Contents

Session Guide

Mindful Moments

Visuals

My Skills for Big Feelings Workbook

INTRODUCTION

Intended Audience

This book was written to help those who work with and care about children, especially children who need help with emotional regulation and anxiety management, or with learning relaxation techniques and coping skills. Whether you are a counselor, educator, psychologist, or social worker, this book aims to help you teach coping and relaxation skills to children in a fun and engaging way. If you are a parent or family member reading this to learn about ways to help your child, you may want to skip to the family resources in the session guide, as that will offer you unique insights from the perspective of a loved one rather than an educator.

The activities in this book were initially developed for use in small and individual counseling settings with children who were experiencing anxiety symptoms. Later, the lessons were expanded upon and implemented on a wider scale in classrooms by both school counselors and teachers. The activities work well when presented in the structured format presented in this book. However, the resources are flexible and can be used in whichever ways are needed to meet the needs of the children.

This program was designed to be secular and includes skills that address the "whole" child, including emotional, cognitive, and physical aspects. This book will guide you in teaching children numerous relaxation skills to cope with their uncomfortable feelings more effectively, utilizing an approach called Feeling-Breath-Thought-Skill (F-B-T-S).

Skills for Big Feelings is written from a relational perspective while drawing on an integrated theoretical framework, including inspiration from cognitive behavioral therapy, expressive arts therapy, yoga, and mindfulness. At the heart of this book is the belief that when families, counselors, teachers, or group facilitators work collaboratively together, by using the same language, modeling, and reinforcing the same skills, the child succeeds.

MY REASONS FOR WRITING THIS BOOK

I feel so passionate about my work with children because I was one of those kids who needed extra emotional support growing up. I was raised by a single mother who had a diagnosis of schizoaffective disorder. My mom was in and out of hospitals during my childhood and adolescence. We were very close, and she loved me dearly. She did the best she could do, but, at times, her mental health challenges impacted her parenting.

At one point, I was in state custody and was placed in kinship foster care. I remember feeling anxious constantly. Sometimes it was about realistic concerns, like worrying that my sneakers were not cool enough or whether or not I would get invited to a party. Other times, my fears were unrealistic, like getting caught in quicksand or getting struck by lightning. I remember my childhood as a time when I was plagued by unhelpful thoughts and big feelings all the time. As a teenager, my anxiety grew more immense and I began having panic attacks. I felt miserable and withdrew from my friends. I had big reactions to small-sized problems, and I felt like I had no control over my emotions.

The educators around me did not pick up on my chronic level of anxiety probably because, like many girls, I internalized my feelings: I did not externalize my feelings by acting out and misbehaving. I tried hard to be a "good girl," which manifested itself in a tendency to be an overachiever who was pretty hard on herself. I wish someone had identified my stressors and struggles early on in my childhood and had offered to teach me skills to manage my anxiety and cope with my feelings more effectively.

When I was around sixteen years old, I started seeing a psychologist who taught me about mindfulness and relaxation skills. Mindfulness as well as a passion for art and music were tools that were extremely impactful to my well-being. I began to slowly discover how to control my anxiety and inner turbulence and I learned from this personal experience that these skills were transformative.

Not surprisingly, since I grew up with a parent with a mental illness and had a time period where I struggled with my own anxieties, I chose to become a counselor myself. The good news is that I am a very content, balanced, and fulfilled person today. The fact that I am a happy and fulfilled person today does not mean that I have transcended emotions and never struggle with uncomfortable feelings or anxiety. However, over the past twenty years, I have worked hard to learn healthy ways to cope with my feelings and I am excited to share the tools I have learned with you.

In my career, I have been working to teach others the coping strategies that I have found to be most useful. I have been working as a counselor in urban public schools since 2007 and, before that, I worked in various settings including outpatient mental health care, hospitals, and group homes. I started practicing guided relaxation, or Mindful Moments, with my students during counseling sessions at an alternative high school in 2007. At the time, it was not a practice that was as widely recognized as it is today. However, since I had my own success with the power of this technique, I shared it on a small scale with my students.

A couple of years later, when I was working at an elementary school, I heard a jarring story about the trauma and violence that a girl I will call Jayda, who was a student at my school, had been exposed to. I was surprised because Jayda was never identified as someone who needed mental health support. She was never brought to my office, probably because she never acted out. I felt guilty that I had not been working with her, and I had not even *realized* she needed my support. I contacted her family to offer assistance, and my mindset shifted that day: I realized then that I needed to take on more of a tier-one, school-wide preventive approach to mental health so that the ones who externalized their behavior and acted out were not the only children who learned these important relaxation skills. I wanted to ensure I was supporting *all* children, even the ones we did not know were struggling. It was then that I began envisioning the creation of *Skills for Big Feelings*, a skills-based mental health curriculum that could be implemented on a much wider scale and used by teachers as well as counselors.

This shift in approach to preventative care has been an essential change in my career. Prior to this, I used to run around my school trying to "put out fires" everywhere. I was on the brink of burnout, and I never felt like I could catch up. This counseling style was not sustainable, and it was fueled by a mistake I made early on in my career: when a child had a problem, I would swoop in and try to be the amazing counselor who was able to calm down and de-escalate the child's feelings. The issue was that *I* became their coping mechanism. This was problematic because it was not empowering to the child at all. I reflected on this and realized that this approach was not effective, and it really needed to change. I needed to shift my focus and empower *all* children by teaching them these important skills. They needed to learn the skills themselves, not have a counselor swoop in to rescue them from their feelings.

My hope is that by implementing interventions earlier and with more children, I will prevent the development of mental health concerns, like the paralyzing anxiety that I experienced as a teen. It is for this reason that I advocate for and truly believe in the power of preventative, tier-one mental health support for all students in schools. All children should be taught so-cial-emotional skills, including the ability to understand their thoughts, feelings, and behav-iors. This is the reason why I made this book skills-based and very practical, not just a clinical guidebook. This book is appropriate for use not only by mental health professionals but also by educators and even parents who want to teach their children skills to relax and cope with their feelings more effectively.

With this preventative framework in mind, I started making small but incremental changes in the schools I worked in. I began to train teachers and other counselors by rolling out the im-plementation of whole-class relaxation skills training to address the needs of more children. I wanted to make sure that we were also including those children who internalized their feel-ings, and not just the ones who were acting out. I knew that many of the children in my school were still in need of supports, just like Jayda and I had been in need, without adults noticing.

The impact of this work has been reaffirmed to me time and time again. For example, one day I received an email from a counselor at a different school that said they were working with an elementary student whose sibling had recently died. When this student came back to school, he said that his cousin, who was a student at my school, had taught him relaxation skills to use when he was feeling sad. I read that email and cried. It was an important moment for me be-cause I realized then that children were out in the community teaching each other these skills, by themselves, on their own time, without any encouragement from me.

> *I am striving to become the person I needed when I was younger.*

I have run various programs, but, to date, Skills for Big Feelings is the most successful group I run. I have had great feedback from the chil-dren, outside counselors, educators, parents, and social workers about how helpful the skills and techniques were. I had the children com-pleting post-group surveys with reaffirming feedback for a few years and when I began to send out the post-group family surveys, I was ex-tremely inspired by the responses of parents and guardians. In fact, the feedback I received from parents about the progress that their children were making at home while participating in this program is what gave me the final push to commit to sharing this work with others on a much larger scale! My hope is to spread these ideas to help more children because, in a take on the words of Ayesha Siddiqi (2013): I am striving to become the person I needed when I was younger.

BEFORE YOU BEGIN: GROUNDWORK AND TOOLS

A Word About Anxiety

My intention with *Skills for Big Feelings* is to use a holistic approach that looks at the whole child and takes into account not just the emotional components, but also the cognitive and physical aspects of the child, while also being developmentally appropriate, structured, and fun. Although the earliest versions of this program were run with a small group of children who were struggling with emotional regulation and anxiety concerns, a child does not need to be diagnosed with any condition to benefit from learning the skills in this book. These skills were found to be beneficial when delivered to larger groups of children on a wider scale, such as in classroom settings. Since each child is unique, not every skill will resonate with every child, and some of the skills may be difficult to master without practice. The workbook offers a variety of skills and, at the conclusion of the twelve sessions, the child will identify the top five skills that they found most useful.

Because anxiety is so commonplace, I believe I only need to discuss it briefly. Nevertheless, it is important to understand how anxiety manifests itself in children. According to the CDC (2019), approximately 4.4 million children in the United States, aged three to seventeen years old, have been diagnosed with an anxiety disorder and these rates are rising over time. One could argue that the actual rate of children suffering with anxiety is probably much higher than 7.1 percent of children, because there are so many children who have not been diagnosed. Research from the CDC (2019) also shows that anxiety is increasing over time for both children and adolescents. Anxiety disorders also have an earlier age of onset, at about eleven years old (Kessler, Berglund, Demler, Jin, Merikangas, and Walters, 2005). In my practice, I commonly see children starting to express anxious behavior at around six or seven years old. Anxiety manifests itself in so many different ways in children and it can often look like oppositional, rigid, and inflexible thinking and behavior. When a child feels anxious, their behavior can be difficult to manage and they may act out. Therefore, it appears that anxiety often underlies a lot of problematic behavior we see in children today.

When children feel anxious, they may experience somatic concerns in their bodies, such as stomachaches or headaches, and they may be very cognitively focused or "in their heads" a lot. Therefore, one of the purposes of using body-based skills, such as stretches, in the workbook is to help children become more aware of what their bodies are doing, which can also help them to come back to the present moment. For example, if a child is truly focused on a body-based skill from the curriculum, such as doing an Ice Cream Twist (page 86) while focusing on their breathing, it will be hard for them to be worried about their math test. In addition, many studies have demonstrated that body movement positively impacts children's cognition, learning, and academic achievement (Chandler and Tricot, 2015).

Breathing techniques have also been proven to "break the anxiety cycle," which is why there are breathing skills taught every week in the children's workbook (Borysenko, 1988, p. 58). Borysenko (1988, p. 58) states that being able to pay attention to your breathing patterns and change them is "one of the most crucial and simplest mind/body skills."

When children misbehave, whether it is because of anxiety or some other issue, it can be extremely stressful for parents, caregivers, and the professionals who work with these children. Caregiver self-care is *so* important and the skills that are written in this book were written in a fun, child-friendly way, but they are also effective for adults! I encourage you to find some healthy coping skills that work well for you. Whether you are a mental health professional, parent, or educator, as a caregiver to children, it will go a long way to model self-care, acceptance, and emotional regulation on a day-to-day basis.

Early on in my career, I was fortunate to discover the work of Dr. Ross Greene from Lives in the Balance. An important concept of Dr. Greene's work is that kids would do well if they could do well. Dr. Greene writes, "If the kid had the skills to exhibit adaptive behavior, he wouldn't be exhibiting challenging behavior. That's because doing well is always preferable to not doing well" (2009). Dr. Greene has various programs about his "Collaborative and Proactive Solutions" model and trains parents and clinicians on how to assess lagging skills and work with children using his framework.

Dr. Greene's model allowed for an important realization that helped me in my own parenting and career: the belief that a child is not purposefully or deliberately acting out and that children, like the rest of us, do the best that they can do in any given moment. Dr. Greene's

Compassionate Communities statement of values notes that "challenging behavior does not come from a place of malice or harmful intent and is instead a way to express frustrations over a lagging skill or an unmet expectation" (n.d.). This is so important to remember because, often, when a child acts out, we may take it personally. Not taking things personally when working with or raising children is an *extremely* helpful skill to develop! For more assistance on this, I refer you to Don Miguel Ruiz's inspiring book, *The Four Agreements: A Practical Guide to Personal Freedom*, which has a chapter entitled "Don't Take Anything Personally" (1999).

Making this mindset shift will allow your attention to pivot away from thinking about what is wrong with a child and move towards a problem-solving approach by figuring out what skills the child needs to learn to be more successful. With this shift, you can focus on figuring out the best way to help the child learn those skills. The purpose of *Skills for Big Feelings* is to teach children how to cope with their uncomfortable feelings more effectively by teaching them relaxation skills and giving them a structure called Feeling-Breath-Thought-Skill, or F-B-T-S for short.

Building Relationships with Presence and Positivity

There are a variety of complex processes that play a role in how people grow and change. Researchers have estimated and are now quantifying what factors work in counseling to make it effective. Interestingly, Thomas (2006) measured contributing factors of therapeutic change and found that therapists and clients vary in how they rate these change factors. His research showed that therapeutic relationship factors, including warmth, empathy, encouragement, and acceptance account for 29–35 percent of change, while a client's hope and expectations account for 27–30 percent of change. This means that you, as the facilitator, can be impactful and make a difference by providing hope and building a positive relationship, whether you are a counselor or not.

If I am running a small pull-out group, before the group begins, I introduce myself to the child. I show the child the room we will be working in and let them ask any questions they may have. This is my chance to start building an important and healing relationship with the child. I always tell them how excited I am to be working with them and try to include a strength I have learned about them from their family or teacher. This positive one-on-one interaction before we start the group is also helpful since transitions can be very stressful for many children.

Knowing what to expect and having the opportunity to ask any questions beforehand, in an individual setting, may help to reduce some fear or worries.

Carl W. Buehner wrote that people "may forget what you said—but they will never forget how you made them feel" (Evans, 1971). It is for this reason that I share my genuine excitement about working with each child individually. I share my enthusiasm about working with them even if I am having a bad day myself because I know that my attitude and actions are so important in the lives of the children I work with. So, my intention is to start *every* interaction with each child in a positive way because making each child feel important helps to foster healing, positive relationships. There is also brain-based research to support this concept. Jordan (2010) found that we enter the world ready to seek connections and "the neurobiological data strongly supports the notion that we need connections to grow and thrive" (p. 95).

In terms of the connection between relationships and resilience, research from the Center on the Developing Child at Harvard University found that childhood resilience involves both supportive relationships and chances for skill-building. They note that no matter what the adversity a child faces, the one shared factor for children who do well is that they all have the "support of at least one stable and committed relationship" with an adult, whether it is a parent, caregiver, or another adult (2015). *You* can be that one stable, committed adult who makes an immense difference in the life of a child!

Charlie Applestein, one of my favorite speakers and author of the book *No Such Thing As A Bad Kid* (1998), wrote about this concept when he talked about working with approximately 250 "very challenging yet wonderful kids, some incredibly difficult to engage…I would like to believe that every one of them woke up every day thinking, 'Mr. A can't wait to see me. I must be his favorite kid.' Was this true? No. Yet I always tried my best to approach all 250" with that enthusiasm (pp. 33–34). In 1972, with a similar notion on how attitude impacts teaching, Haim Ginott wrote about classroom climate and how he came to realize that as the teacher, *he* was the decisive element in his classroom. He wrote that it was his "daily mood that makes the weather" and how his own approach with his students had an incredible "power to make a child's life miserable or joyous" (pp. 15-16).

Likewise, Brené Brown, Ph.D., LMSW (2019) wrote how Toni Morrison's words about being positive with children made her a better mother:

> Morrison explained that it's interesting to watch what happens when a child walks into a room. She asked, "Does your face light up?" She explained, "When

my children used to walk in the room when they were little, I looked at them to see if they had buckled their trousers or if their hair was combed or if their socks were up. You think your affection and your deep love is on display because you're caring for them. It's not. When they see you, they see the critical face. What's wrong now?"

Her advice was simple, but paradigm-shifting for me. She said:

"Let your face speak what's in your heart. When they walk in the room my face says I'm glad to see them. It's just as small as that, you see?"

Similarly, the beloved Fred Rogers, in a 1997 interview with Charlie Rose, talked about being mindful in your interactions with others:

We get so wrapped up in numbers in our society. The most important thing is that we are able to be one-to-one, you and I with each other at the moment. If we can be present to the moment with the person that we happen to be with, that's what's important (Rose, 1997).

This advice about relationships, whether it's aimed at mothers, teachers, or counselors, and whether it comes from 1972 or 2019, all rings true and has the same central message for us: be present, stable, committed, and positive with children. This cumulative advice has been vital in my career and in my personal life. For example, even if I do not feel 100 percent excited or engaged because of my own issues such as physical pain, fatigue, or stress, I try my best to stay mindful and present with the child I am working with, not letting my personal distress impact those interactions. I try to be upbeat and positive with them. The influence of this strategy alone has been powerful. Please note that I am not encouraging you to be inauthentic or fake with the children you work with. I am, however, encouraging you to shift your attention to the positive and the present moment, which are both strategies we teach in *Skills for Big Feelings*. When you begin to practice this, it will be impactful, both in your career and personal life.

Structure

The session guide is comprised of twelve sessions that build upon each other. Each session is made up of two guided relaxation scripts, called Mindful Moments, an activity, and three weekly skills.

The activities in Session One introduce children to the concept of naming and accepting all feelings. Session Two teaches children about the concept of triggers and introduces them to the Feeling-Breath-Thought-Skill framework. Session Three is devoted to learning about helpful and unhelpful thoughts, and, in Session Four, children learn how to change unhelpful thoughts into more helpful thoughts. In Session Five, children are introduced to a scale to measure their challenges, and, in Session Six, they learn how to evaluate whether or not their responses match the challenges. Sessions Seven, Eight, and Nine teach children how to use visualization, synchronizing their breath with words and positive self-talk. Session Ten examines the importance of making mistakes and identifying each child's support system. Session Eleven is focused on mindfulness and gratitude, and Session Twelve is the closure session which focuses on the concept of control and allows each child to identify their top five favorite skills.

"If children feel safe, they can take risks, ask questions, make mistakes, learn to trust, share their feelings, and grow." (Kohn, 1999, p. 239)

The Skills for Big Feelings sessions are set up to be structured, but, if you are limited on time and find that there is too much content to fit into one setting, feel free to use the materials in a way that works for your schedule and the children you are working with. I found that keeping a consistent structure has proven to be very beneficial and helps the children feel safe. If you are running a shorter session (30 minutes or less), you might want to consider either extending the sessions to more than twelve weeks, having the children complete the weekly activity at home in between sessions, or doing a little bit each day. The outline of a typical session is as follows:

- Opening practice

- Review agreements

- Visual schedule

- Mindful Moment and Feelings Check

- Activity

- Practice and color the three weekly skills

- Mindful Moment and Feelings Check

- Closing practice

- Send-home family resource (if applicable)

Opening and Closing Practices

You can help children feel safe by using consistent opening and closing practices in group work since they create containment and structure. It is important to develop an initial and closing practice, which stays the same throughout the entire duration of the group. I like to think of these practices as brief bookends that carve out the time and space of the group. Your practices can be short and simple as long as they are consistent. As part of your opening and closing practices, it can be helpful to establish and teach your routines and expectations. For example, you might want the children to know how you would like them to enter and exit your room.

One of my opening practices includes having the children "press pause" before entering my office by placing a hand on their bellies and taking a slow, deep breath in through their nose and out through their mouth. I then remind them that I want them to walk slowly into the room and choose a cushion to sit on. Next, I show a visual of our group agreements and we review our visual schedule.

Ideas for Opening Practices

- Before entering the room, have children "press pause" by placing a hand on their belly and taking a slow, deep breath in through their nose and out through their mouth. This can also be used as a closing practice.

- Show a visual of the group agreements and review them together.

- Review the visual schedule for the session or the day.

- Ring a bell or chime with a calming sound. It's helpful to use a bell that starts loud and slowly gets quieter. Have the children listen to the sound of the bell while breathing.

13

Alternatively, they can raise their hand when they notice the bell has stopped ringing completely. This can also be used as a closing practice.

- Do a Feelings Check by passing around an object, such as a ball, and using a sentence starter such as "I feel . . ." This can also be used as a closing practice.

- Do a Feelings Check by having the children use a clothespin to identify what emotion they are feeling in the present moment on a chart. This can also be used as a closing practice.

- Have each child share a body movement and/or sound to represent how they are feeling in the present moment. The other children, then, mirror it back to them. This can also be used as a closing practice.

- Have each child share a stretch or movement that feels good to their body and the other children repeat it back. This can also be used as a closing practice.

- Do a Feelings Check by passing around an object, such as a ball, and have each person share their mood by giving a weather report. For example, "Today I am feeling sunny because it's my birthday!" or "Today I am feeling foggy with thunderstorms because I have a headache." This can also be used as a closing practice.

Ideas for Closing Practices

Children thrive when they have routines, responsibility, structure, and agreements because they feel safe.

- Share a compliment with someone in the group. The group may benefit from some sentence-starter prompts or encouragement to give "inside compliments" rather than compliments about someone's appearance, such as "I really liked what you said about . . ."

- Pass around an object, such as a ball, and say something you learned, enjoyed, or found challenging today.

- Hold hands and pass a squeeze around the group.

- Share something you are grateful for today.

- As a group, create a mantra to say together such as, "We are respectful, responsible, safe, kind, and calm!" or "We can do anything!"

- Have the children visualize themselves successfully transitioning back into the outside environment, such as their classroom, hospital, or group home.

- Have a box or jar available with positive quotes or affirmations and give each child the option to pull out a quote and read the positive words or phrase aloud.

Agreements

Children are inundated with rules wherever they go. I begin the first session by establishing our group rules, or agreements. I prefer to use the term "agreements" rather than "rules," because the term "rules" implies compliance with authority figures whereas agreements are co-created, mutually agreed upon, and are more cooperative. I tell the children that these are the agreements we make with each other to have a great group. At the first group session, I empower the children to discuss which agreements they would like to have. The children may need some help with this activity depending on their age or developmental level. If the children are young, you can use a visual, or body movement to represent each agreement. Since we do a lot of stretches in each session, be sure to include an agreement about doing only what feels good or comfortable for each child's body. In the visuals section, you will find a poster for you to write your agreements on.

Review the agreements at the start of every session as part of your opening practice. Your agreements will vary based on the type of group, members of the group, and the age of the children in the group. Some common group agreements may include the following: confidentiality; being safe, kind, and respectful; having one person talk at a time; staying on topic; and only doing what feels good for one's body.

Visual Schedule

Many children benefit from knowing what to expect. A useful tool to assist with this need is to include a visual schedule of the plan for the day. This is also helpful to use when children struggle with transitions. You can create your own visual schedule with a dry-erase board or use Our Plan for Today in the visuals section.

After reviewing the visual schedule, you can show the self-scan visual, and do a Mindful Moment, followed by a Feelings Check.

Self-Scan

Instead of telling children what to do with their bodies and correcting them with directives like "sit in your chair right," "stop stamping your feet," or "don't touch that," you can teach children how to do a self-scan, or how to look at their own bodies to see if it is doing what is expected. This helps children develop self-awareness skills, which is one of CASEL's core social-emotional learning competencies (2019).

Jessica Minahan, author of two wonderful books, *The Behavior Code* and *The Behavior Code Companion,* writes about a similar strategy but uses the term body-check. This strategy is also more aligned with a trauma-sensitive approach, and it helps children feel more in control. Minahan explains that "each body-check prompt is a crucial teaching moment where the student learns self-regulation and self-monitoring skills and moves toward independence" (2014, p. 94). Before doing a Mindful Moment, after doing an active activity (e.g., F-B-T-S Balloon Bop), or even before transitioning to walking in the hallway, I always prompt the children to do a self-scan.

Children who are sensitive and might ordinarily become upset or dysregulated if you give them a directive or correction tend to cope much better with this type of reminder. I have not yet had a child who became upset when I asked them to do a self-scan. To help you teach this concept, I have included a self-scan visual for you.

Mindful Moments and Feelings Check

Mindful Moments, a secular practice that many will benefit from, are guided relaxation scripts. We start each Mindful Moment with a self-scan. My intention while writing these scripts was to use invitational language in an attempt to be more trauma-sensitive. Please note that due to this choice of language, the length of the scripts may be too long for some of your children, especially if they are younger or have not experienced guided relaxation scripts before. So, feel free to shorten the scripts as needed. I have provided brief versions of some of the scripts including those for muscle relaxation, gentle body movements, and body scans on my website: http://www.wholechildcounseling.com/helpful-place.

Kearney and Simpson (2020) write about teaching mindfulness to people who have experienced trauma. They suggest building a "container of trust" (p. 74) first, which the positive presence and the structure help provide, as well as using "language in the form of an invitation as a way of promoting empowerment and choice" (p. 90). To learn more about trauma-sensitive mindfulness practices, I refer you to David Treleaven's book *Trauma-Sensitive Mindfulness: Practices for Safe and Transformative Healing* (2018). Treleaven (2018) describes observable cues of dysregulated arousal and identifies five principles for trauma-sensitive mindfulness. He also includes suggestions to help people have who experienced trauma understand and stay within their window of tolerance.

It is important to remember that this may be the first time the children experience a guided relaxation script or Mindful Moment, so make sure you let them know what to expect and give them some choices. For example, some children might not feel comfortable closing their eyes and that's okay! You can give them the option to soften their gaze instead or say, "If you feel comfortable, you can…" At first, the children might need an example from you of what softening their gaze or looking down at their nose looks and feels like; otherwise, some children might get goofy and start crossing their eyes. Before you embark on your first Mindful Moment, you will also want to remind the children about the goals you are working on together while practicing Mindful Moments.

When reading the scripts, try to use a soothing, calm tone. Read slowly and be sure to pause where appropriate. You can also ad-lib as needed. For example, if a child is breathing out very loudly and you think it might be distracting to others, you might say "remember to take quiet breaths." Or, if you hear noises outside the room, you can add a comment such as "let any sounds you hear fade away into the background." As the children get more comfortable with the process, you can also give them longer periods of silence, but you will want to keep those pauses brief at first.

After the Mindful Moment, if time allows, it is helpful to do a Feelings Check to gauge how the children's experience was, especially when first introducing this technique. It is helpful for the facilitator to model what is expected during the Feelings Check by saying something like "I haven't done a Mindful Moment in a while, so that felt very relaxing to me. But I was also a little distracted today and thinking about some other things. I know that with some time and practice, the 'Mindful Moments' will get easier for me again." During the Feelings Check, it is important to emphasize the fact that *all* feelings are valid and welcome in the space. We want to model being nonjudgmental and be sure we don't label emotions as positive or negative, good or bad.

Activity and Coloring the Three Weekly Skills

After our Mindful Moment and Feelings Check, we do our daily activity and move on to learn and practice the three weekly skills by coloring them. From my perspective, it is important to give the children a chance to color the three skills that they learn each week as coloring can produce a mindful state. Coloring has also been proven to have positive effects in people, including "anxiety reduction and…higher perseverance" (Eaton and Tieber, 2017, p. 42). By having the children color the skills, my hope is that it will also help them visually learn and recall the skills more easily.

I always encourage the children to be creative and color the pictures however they want to. I remind them that there are no right or wrong ways to color because the special workbook belongs to *them*. They might also want to draw their own versions of the skills, which I also encourage. My hope is that this also gives them some ownership over the skills. While the children are coloring or drawing, we sometimes chat as a group. Although, with some groups, the children can become so engrossed in their coloring that they don't want to talk, and that is totally okay too! It is important to meet them wherever they are. If you, as the facilitator, decide to color while the children are coloring, this is a perfect opportunity to model making mistakes and measuring challenges! I try not to color or draw too "perfectly," as the children tend to compare their artwork to mine.

I typically have the children use crayons but if working with older children, you may prefer to offer a choice between crayons and colored pencils. It takes a lot longer to color with colored pencils, so if you are using them, you will want to plan your time accordingly. I chose to limit the media choices to crayons and colored pencils, because I found that if you give children too many choices, it can cause them to feel overwhelmed. I don't use markers in the workbook because I print the pages double-sided to save paper. I try to stock up on special glitter crayons and put them in plastic crayon cases, so that each child has their own special crayon box. These are little touches that are not necessary, but the children appreciate this attention to detail.

In my Skills for Big Feelings groups, we sit on cushions on the floor, so we use clipboards to lean on while coloring. You can purchase outdoor patio cushions on sale after the summer season. I prefer using outdoor cushions to sit on because they are more durable. When I run the Skills for Big Feelings program in larger groups, such as in a whole classroom setting, each child works at their own table or desk.

The reason I use colored pencils and crayons as the main medium for this group is because they are resistive or dry, which allows for "cognitive control and safety" (Ichiki and Hinz, 2015, as cited in Hinz, 2020, p. 28). This dry media also elicits "feelings of control" which "can decrease feelings of anxiety early in the therapeutic relationship" (Regev and Snir, 2018, as cited in Hinz, 2020 p. 29). Children struggling with emotional regulation often want to control things because they may feel out of control, which is why one of the activities in Session Twelve is devoted to the concept of control. Children should feel empowered and develop an internal locus of control rather than an external locus of control, which means that one usually anticipates that "outcomes are the result of external forces rather than one's own behavior or competence" (Platt, Williams, and Ginsburg, 2016, p. 24).

Closure

We close the group by doing another Mindful Moment and a Feelings Check. We do our closing practice, and then I hand out the family resource, if it is applicable to that particular setting. Please note that the family resources were originally developed for children with anxiety, so they may not be appropriate for your setting (such as in classrooms.) If you choose not to send the family resource home, you might consider sending a copy of the three weekly skills the children learned that week, so they can refer to them for practice.

At the end of the session, I remind the children how I want them to exit the room. For example, after the closing practice, I call their names, one at a time, have them put away their cushions, and ask them to line up. When working with young children, it's useful to have visual markers in your space for where you want them to line up, especially when they are first learning the routines. I find it helpful to use painter's tape to mark a space on the floor where they should line up.

Informed Consent

If I am running a small group in a public school, I reach out to the parents beforehand to converse with them about the group, including what to expect and the objectives. I have found this to be helpful because I can answer any questions they may have on the phone. I then send a letter home, like the sample below, with an attached consent form. I know some counselors may use passive informed consent, such as opt-out forms, but I don't prefer to use them for small-group work. Ideally, the parents will be active collaborators and practicing the skills with their children at home on a weekly basis.

Date:__/__/__

Dear Parent/Guardian of _____,

Your child has been recommended to participate in a 12-week group called "Skills for Big Feelings." This group will meet once a week and will work on teaching your child ways to manage his/her feelings more effectively. Each week, we will be practicing breathing, stretching, and various relaxation skills. This group is a wonderful opportunity for children to build confidence in themselves, learn valuable skills, and, ultimately, enhance their personal, social, and emotional growth.

I am looking forward to working with you and your child. I am a firm believer that collaboration between school and home is instrumental to your child's success and that you, as the caregiver, are an expert when it comes to understanding your child's needs. Each week, your child will bring home a Skills for Big Feelings Family Resource, which will tell you what we learned about that week and give you three skills to practice and ways to reinforce the lessons at home. If you should ever have any insights, questions, or concerns please feel free to contact me. I can be reached at . . .

If you would like for your child to participate in this group, please complete the attached form and return it to me by . . .

Sincerely,

Name, Title

Standards and Competencies

The Collaborative for Academic, Social, and Emotional Learning (2019) has identified five core competencies of social-emotional learning. The main competencies that are addressed within this curriculum include self-awareness, such as identifying feelings, and self-management, such as managing stress. In addition, the American School Counselor Association has identified mindsets and behavior standards for student success (2014), several of which are related to the content covered in *Skills for Big Feelings*.

Depending on how you are using this book and where you are facilitating the sessions, you may need to write objectives for Individual Education Plans (IEPs) or treatment-plan goals. You want to collect baseline data before writing your goals so that you can make sure they are realistic and achievable. For example, if a child cannot currently name any coping skills, you do not want to say that they will be able to independently identify and demonstrate the use of fifteen coping skills within three months. You want your objectives to be S.M.A.R.T., which means they are (S)pecific, (M)easurable, (A)chievable, (R)elevant, and (T)ime-bound (Bjerke and Renger, 2017).

There is a data-collection sheet available for you to use in the visuals section. To use this data-collection sheet, write down the skill or objective at the top, along with the date, and write each child's name in the left column. If a child answers correctly, place a check mark in the data column. If a child answers correctly with assistance (e.g., if they ask for help, which is encouraged), underline the check mark in the data column. If a child answers incorrectly, put an X in the data column and if a child does not answer, put a question mark in the data column. Tally the correct number of answers out of the total number in the right column to calculate a fraction or percentage. Examples of some S.M.A.R.T. objectives that align with the lessons in this book are listed below. For more information on writing social-emotional treatment plan and IEP objectives, please refer to my book: *Social-Emotional IEP and Treatment Plan Objectives: S.M.A.R.T. Treatment Planning Made Easy.*

IEP and Treatment Plan Objectives

- To increase knowledge and use of coping skills by [Date], [Name] will be able to identify [number] or more coping skills, [given conditions/level of support: independently, with fading staff support, with visuals, etc.], as demonstrated by data log.

Example: To increase knowledge and use of coping skills by February 5, 2024, Tina will be able to identify 5 or more coping skills, given direct teaching and fading staff support, as demonstrated by data log.

- To increase knowledge and use of coping skills by [Date], [Name] will be able to identify the four components of F-B-T-S (Feeling-Breath-Thought-Skill), [given conditions/level of support: independently, with fading staff support, with visuals, etc.], as demonstrated by data log.

  Example: To increase knowledge and use of coping skills by April 16, 2024, Juan will be able to identify the four components of F-B-T-S (Feeling-Breath-Thought-Skill), with visual supports, as demonstrated by data log.

- To increase problem-solving, critical thinking, and the application of coping skills by [Date], [Name] will be able to identify the four components of F-B-T-S (Feeling-Breath-Thought-Skill) and apply the four components to a role-play scenario, [given conditions/level of support: independently, with fading staff support, with visuals, etc.], in [number] out of [number] scenarios, as demonstrated by data log and observation.

  Example: To increase problem-solving, critical thinking, and the application of coping skills by May 3, 2025, Carla will be able to identify the four components of F-B-T-S (Feeling-Breath-Thought-Skill) and apply the four components to a role-play scenario, with fading staff supports, in 3 out of 5 scenarios, as demonstrated by data log and observation.

- To increase generalization of problem-solving, critical thinking, and coping skills by [Date], [Name] will be able to identify the four components of F-B-T-S (Feeling-Breath-Thought-Skill) and apply the four components to a real-life situation, [given conditions/level of support: independently, with fading staff support, with visuals, etc.], in [number] out of [number] scenarios, as demonstrated by practice log, counselor observation, and parent/teacher report.

  Example: To increase generalization of problem-solving, critical thinking, and coping skills by April 9, 2024, Antonio will be able to identify the four components of F-B-T-S (Feeling-Breath-Thought-Skill) and apply the four components to a real-life situation, independently, in 4 out of 5 scenarios, as demonstrated by practice log, counselor observation, and parent/teacher report.

- To increase self-awareness and emotional identification in a [type of setting], [Name] will be able to state how they feel, [given conditions/level of support: independently, with fading staff support, with visuals, etc.], in [number] out of [number] scenarios by [Date], as evidenced by data log and observation.

  Example: To increase self-awareness and emotional identification in a small, structured group setting, Tobi will be able to state how they feel, using visual supports, in 3 out of 5 scenarios by March 11, 2024, as evidenced by data log and counselor observation.

- To enhance self-awareness and self-management when given a prompt from the [group facilitator title], [Name] will be able to demonstrate what it means to do a self-scan by looking at their body and readjusting as needed, [given conditions/level of support: independently, with fading staff support, with visuals, etc.], in [number] out of [number] scenarios by [Date], as evidenced by observation and data log.

  Example: To enhance self-awareness and self-management when given a prompt from the counselor, Regi will be able to demonstrate what it means to do a self-scan by looking at his body and readjusting as needed, given visual cues, in 4 out of 5 scenarios by May 18, 2024, as evidenced by counselor observation and data log.

- To increase self-awareness skills by [Date], [Name] will be able to state [number] or more bodily symptoms they experience when they are feeling [emotion], [given conditions/level of support: independently, with fading staff support, with visuals, etc.] as demonstrated by data log and observation.

  Example: To increase self-awareness by June 22, 2024, Hector will be able to state at least 3 bodily symptoms he experiences when he is feeling anxious, with fading staff support, as demonstrated by data log and observation.

- To increase emotional vocabulary skills by [Date], [Name] will be able to state [number] or more feelings, [given conditions/level of support: independently, with fading staff support, with visuals, etc.], as demonstrated by data log.

  Example: To increase emotional vocabulary skills by October 29, 2024, Gavin will be able to state 10 or more feelings using visuals supports, as demonstrated by data log.

- To increase emotional identification and social skills by [Date], [Name] will be able to state what a person may be feeling in a given situation or role-play scenario, [given conditions/level of support: independently, with fading staff support, with visuals, etc.], in [number] out of [number] opportunities, as demonstrated by data log and observation.

  Example: To increase emotional identification and social skills by May 3, 2024, Harry will be able to state what a person may be feeling in a given situation or role-play scenario, independently, in 9 out of 10 opportunities, as demonstrated by data log and observation.

- To increase self-awareness and emotional regulation skills by [Date], [Name] will be able to state [number] or more triggers for [feeling], [given conditions/level of support: independently, with fading staff support, with visuals, etc.], as demonstrated by data log and observation.

  Example: To increase self-awareness and emotional regulation skills by January 4, 2024, Sammi will be able to state 3 or more triggers for feeling frustrated or angry, with fading adult support, as demonstrated by data log and observation.

- To increase self-awareness, metacognition, and emotional regulation by [Date], [Name] will be able to identify the difference between helpful and unhelpful thoughts, [given conditions/level of support: independently, with fading staff support, with visuals, etc.], in [number] out of [number] scenarios, as demonstrated by data log.

  Example: To increase self-awareness, metacognition, and emotional regulation by June 4, 2024, Katia will be able to identify the difference between helpful and unhelpful thoughts, independently, in 4 out of 5 scenarios, as demonstrated by data log.

- To increase self-awareness, metacognition, and emotional regulation by [Date], [Name] will be able to identify [number] or more helpful and [number] or more unhelpful thoughts that they experience, [given conditions/level of support: independently, with fading staff support, with visuals, etc.], as demonstrated by data log and observation.

  Example: To increase self-awareness, metacognition, and emotional regulation by September 5, 2024, Zoe will be able to identify 5 or more helpful and 5 or more unhelpful thoughts that she experiences, with fading support, as demonstrated by data log and observation.

- To decrease anxiety and increase self-awareness, metacognition, and emotional regulation by [Date], [Name] will be able to [given conditions/level of support: independently, with fading staff support, with visuals, etc.] change [number] out of [number] unhelpful thoughts into more helpful thoughts, as demonstrated by data log and observation.

  Example: To decrease anxiety and increase self-awareness, metacognition, and emotional regulation by October 8, 2024, Aden will be able to independently change 4 out of 5 unhelpful thoughts into more helpful thoughts, as demonstrated by data log and observation.

- To help increase an internal locus of control and self-awareness by [Date], [Name] will be able to, [given conditions/level of support: independently, with fading staff support, with visuals, etc.], explain the 3 components of the CBT triangle and how they are connected, as demonstrated by data log and observation.

  Example: To help increase an internal locus of control and self-awareness by November 24, 2024, Evan, utilizing visual support, will be able to explain the 3 components of the CBT triangle and how they are connected, as demonstrated by data log and observation.

- To increase emotional regulation and decrease feelings of [emotion] by [Date], [Name] will be able to identify [number] or more positive or helpful thoughts, [given conditions/level of support: independently, with fading staff support, with visuals, etc.], as demonstrated by data log and observation.

  Example: To increase emotional regulation and decrease anxious or depressive feelings by January 5, 2024, Jamie will be able to identify 5 or more positive or helpful thoughts, with fading support, as demonstrated by data log and observation.

- To increase problem-solving skills by [Date], [Name] will be able to accurately measure challenges using a scale, [given conditions/level of support: independently, with fading staff support, with visuals, etc.] in [number] out of [number] scenarios as demonstrated by data log and observation.

Example: To increase problem-solving skills by February 18, 2024, Selma will be able to accurately measure challenges using a scale, given direct teaching and visual supports, in 3 out of 5 scenarios, as demonstrated by data log and observation.

- To increase problem-solving and emotional regulation skills by [Date], [Name] will be able to [given conditions/level of support: independently, with fading staff support, with visuals, etc.] match the size of a challenge with the size of a response on a scale in [number] out of [number] scenarios as demonstrated by data log and observation.

Example: To increase problem-solving and emotional regulation skills by July 3, 2024, Mike will be able to independently match the size of a challenge with the size of a response on a scale in 4 out of 5 scenarios, as demonstrated by data log and observation.

- To increase relaxation and emotional regulation and to decrease feelings of [emotion] by [Date], [Name] will be able to successfully utilize visualization techniques to envision their relaxing happy place and be able to use [number] or more descriptive words to describe their relaxing happy place, [given conditions/level of support: independently, with fading staff support, with visuals, etc.], as demonstrated by data log and observation.

Example: To increase relaxation and emotional regulation and to decrease feelings of anxiety by May 28, 2024, Jenny will be able to successfully utilize visualization techniques to envision her relaxing happy place and be able to use 3 or more descriptive words to describe her relaxing happy place, with fading support, as demonstrated by data log and observation.

- To increase relaxation coping skills and decrease feelings of [emotion] by [Date], [Name] will be able to, [given conditions/level of support: independently, with fading staff support, with visuals, etc.], identify a relaxing word and synchronize it with their breathing, as demonstrated by data log and observation.

Example: To increase relaxation coping skills and decrease feelings of anxiety, by September 25, 2024, Logan will be able to identify a relaxing word and synchronize it with his breathing, with fading counselor support, as demonstrated by data log and observation.

- To increase relaxation coping skills and decrease feelings of [emotion] by [Date], [Name] will be able to, [given conditions/level of support: independently, with fading staff support, with visuals, etc.], state a positive self-talk phrase to utilize when they are feeling [emotion], as demonstrated by data log and observation.

  Example: To increase relaxation coping skills and decrease feelings of anxiety by October 7, 2024, Olivia will be able to independently state a positive self-talk phrase to utilize when she is feeling frustrated or anxious, as demonstrated by data log and observation.

- To increase awareness of supportive relationships by [Date], [Name] will be able to identify [number] or more supportive people across [number] or more different settings, [given conditions/level of support: independently, with fading staff support, with visuals, etc.], as demonstrated by data log and observation.

  Example: To increase awareness of supportive relationships by November 8, 2024, Marcia will be able to identify 2 or more supportive people across 2 different settings (home and school), independently, as demonstrated by data log and observation.

- To help increase an internal locus of control and self-awareness by [Date], [Name] will be able to, [given conditions/level of support: independently, with fading staff support, with visuals, etc.], identify [number] or more things they have control over, as demonstrated by data log and observation.

  Example: To help increase an internal locus of control and self- awareness by June 8, 2024, Heaven will be able to, with visual supports, identify 3 or more things she has control over, as demonstrated by data log and observation.

Data Collection

In addition to collecting data on specific objectives for IEPs or treatment planning, you can also collect data on your children's progress in general. This will help you evaluate and re-assess your program to see what type of changes you could make to improve your outcomes. The American School Counselor Association has published a book called *Making Data Work* (2018) and offers an ASCA U School Counseling Data Specialist online training (ASCA, n.d.). You can also consider using some of the data from the post-group surveys to measure the children's progress on their objectives or treatment plan goals.

If you are in a more clinical setting and credentialed to do so, you might consider using a baseline and post-group anxiety measure such as the "Spence Children's Anxiety Scale," which is available online for free (Spence, 1994).

You can also share your data with stakeholders, as it can be a useful tool to advocate for your program and appropriate usage of your time. I know from personal experience that it can make you feel vulnerable to put surveys out there, but I really encourage you to take this leap! As I mentioned, receiving parental feedback is what gave me the push that I needed to commit to finishing this book. Although I felt a little vulnerable each time I put a survey out there, I have found time and time again that collecting this data is very reaffirming to my work. In the visuals section, you will see a sample of both child and parent post-group surveys. You can also consider creating teacher surveys or collecting pre-group and post-group data to compare results.

Successful Implementation Tips

- It can be hard for children to stop coloring. Always give the children a transition warning and a countdown for when they will need to stop coloring or drawing. Then, ask them to find a comfortable place to stop coloring. If possible, consider using a visual timer.

- When doing the Feelings Checks, try to encourage the children to discuss how they are feeling in the *present* moment.

- Count the 10-second stretches aloud. As the group progresses, you can increase the number of seconds you practice for, if it feels appropriate.

- The activity worksheets have words that are numbered, so, if you have early-readers, you can have them point to the number and read it aloud.

- If you have children who have difficulty with motor tasks, when you have activities that need a ball, O-balls are a great choice because they are easier to catch.

- During check-ins or sharing times, *never* force a child to share. If they aren't comfortable speaking, they should always be allowed to pass.

- If a child says they are too scared or anxious to join the group, ask them to try it one time and then give them the freedom to make a decision.

- If the children are getting very off-topic with conversations, or if they are talking for a very long time during check-ins, let them know you will give them time to chat while they color their skills, but, for now, they should try to stay focused on whatever you are working on.

- Do not feel pressured to cram in every single activity in each session. If the timeline of the sessions does not work for you, then be flexible and change it. If you are stressed and rush to make sure you finish all the content each week, the children will pick up on your feelings and will not be able to relax as deeply. I like to have extra content on hand because I prefer to be over-prepared. You can see what works best for you, such as experimenting with extending the group time or the number or frequency of sessions if needed.

- If possible, when working with small groups in a school setting, try to schedule your groups first thing in the morning to ensure they are carried out with fidelity.

- Tell the children that the brain is kind of like a muscle and needs exercise and practice to get stronger, which will encourage their participation in some of the more difficult skills or Mindful Moments.

- Reinforce the idea that they should not be judgmental or mad at themselves if some of the skills or the Mindful Moments are difficult for them. Model being gentle, kind, and nonjudgmental to yourself. Appropriately talk to them about your personal experiences or struggles with Mindful Moments, such as if thoughts pop into your mind while you are trying to focus on your breath.

- We always want to be trauma-sensitive in our work, so never force children to close their eyes or participate in something they aren't comfortable with. We always use language that is empowering to children. For example, "when you are ready, I invite you to…" or "when you feel comfortable, you can…"

- You can use real-life situations that happen while you are working with the children to model making mistakes, measuring challenges, and using the Feeling-Breath-Thought-Skill strategy.

Large Group or Whole Classroom Implementation

- This guide can be adapted for use in a variety of settings.

- Rather than engaging in a 30–50 minute session once a week, some teachers or facilitators have found it helpful to divide the sessions into smaller chunks and complete a shorter portion each day. Some teachers have incorporated the curriculum into their everyday teaching as part of their daily morning meeting by spreading out the content throughout the week. For example, you might do an introduction to the week's content on Monday, a Mindful Moment on Tuesday, a workbook activity on Wednesday, the three skills on Thursday, and a Mindful Moment on Friday. Each day, you can practice the skills that were previously learned throughout the day, such as before or after a transition.

- Opening and closing practices may be as simple as turning off or dimming the lights. Alternatively, in a whole-class setting in which you are portioning the sessions daily, you might not use these components.

- You may not need to create separate agreements, because you already have classroom rules established.

- If you are implementing these activities during different parts of the day (e.g., part of a session during morning meeting and part at the end of the day), you might skip the visual schedule.

- In a large class, you might not have time to do a Feelings Check. However, it might be helpful to do one the first several times you practice the Mindful Moments.

- In Session Four, if there is not enough space for each child to lay down, you might have to be creative and alter the way you teach the Buddy Breath skill (page 61). You might consider having each child place a hand on their bellies while sitting in their chair instead.

If Time Allows

- Have each child share one skill or stretch, and let the other group members repeat it back together.

- Remember to plan for early finishers. I always encourage my early finishers to decorate the front and back covers of their workbook. You can also add some blank pages into the back of the workbooks. Some children enjoy drawing their inner experiences during their Mindful Moments, so giving them these blank pages is helpful.

- Practice the new skills and review the old skills. Ideally, you will do this several times each week. You can then review the skills from previous weeks by calling out the names and having the children recall and practice those skills as well.

Workbook Assembly

If possible, I recommend copying the front cover of the workbook on cardstock and adding a blank sheet of cardstock for the back cover to make it more durable. It is also helpful to add some blank pages in the back for drawing or early finishers. If you don't want to photocopy the pages in this book, you can go to https://www.wholechildcounseling.com/helpful-place for exclusive access to a printable version.

The workbook does not have page numbers written on it, so, if you are binding it as a book format, you might consider having the children add page numbers or writing them in yourself before photocopying it. This may make it easier for them to find which activity you are referring to.

You can bind the workbook in many different ways. Here are some examples:

- Use a brad paper fastener

- Staple the pages together

- Use a spiral or comb binding machine

- Three-hole punch the pages and put them in a three-ring binder or in a presentation cover

- Hole punch the top left corner of the workbook pages and use a loose binder ring to fasten the pages together

If you are using *Skills for Big Feelings* during remote learning, please do not place any copies of the book or workbook on a website that is searchable. The workbook and family pages can be emailed to students or families or posted for your own students on a password-protected learning management system. Visit http://www.wholechildcounseling.com for interactive digital options.

Graduation Letter

The *Skills for Big Feelings* curriculum can be implemented into an ongoing group. However, if it is run in the twelve-week format as presented here, you should let the children know, in the first session, that the group will last for twelve weeks. Termination, or the process of ending the group, can be difficult for the children, and even for the group facilitator. In my experience, the children *love* the group so much that they often beg to continue. Honestly, I have so much fun with the children that I often do not want the sessions to end either! I sometimes have to remind myself that I am empowering the children to learn the skills and make positive changes in their own lives and I do not want them to stay dependent on me. This is one of the reasons the children are asked to practice the skills at home with their families.

I recommend discussing termination again in the sixth session, which is the halfway point and then bringing it up weekly starting at the tenth session. Give the children time to process their feelings about the group ending. I never use the clinical term "termination" with the children. I call it graduation, and I tell them how proud I am that they are graduating and have learned so many skills. I let them know they will get to bring home their special workbooks and teach someone in their family all the skills they learned. During the last session, the children fill out post-group surveys. I also call all the parents and send the following letter along with the parent post-group survey.

Date: __/__/__

Dear Parent/Guardian of _____,

We had a wonderful Skills for Big Feelings group, and I am excited to share with you that your child has graduated! I would appreciate it if you could please fill out the attached survey and return it to me. You can keep it anonymous if you would like.

Each child is coming home with their Skills for Big Feelings workbook today, which contains all of the skills they learned in the sessions. Your child's home-work is to teach someone in their family these skills. Please know that they don't need to teach you the whole book in one sitting, but it would be great to set aside some time each day to practice and reinforce these relaxation skills with them. Common times for practice are right before bedtime and in the morning before school.

The more your child practices these skills and knows how to use them, the easier it will be for them to access them when they are facing uncomfortable feelings. By having your child teach you these skills, you will be able to model using them and remind your child to use them when you see them becoming upset. Giving them a structured choice between two or three skills to practice is helpful and may increase the likelihood of follow-through.

Thank you for allowing me to be part of your child's social-emotional learning. I really enjoyed running this group. Please do not hesitate to call me if you have any questions or concerns moving forward. I can be reached at . . .

With gratitude,

Name
Title

SESSION GUIDE

Facilitator Notes

In the session guide that follows, I have described what you will say as the facilitator to lead the sessions. The instructions for you are italicized. Please don't feel like you need to read the sessions verbatim or remember exactly everything that is written down for each session. This is a guidebook with suggestions. Be authentic and bring your own unique personality to this work!

In addition, it is important to note that the family resources might not be appropriate for every setting. They were written particularly for parents and guardians of children who were learning to manage anxiety. Therefore, if presenting the program to a whole classroom, or in a larger setting, they might not be appropriate to send home.

I suggest preparing all the materials by printing all of the visuals and family resources in advance. You can store all the objects that will be used weekly in a bin or box. You might find it helpful to use sticky notes or a bookmark to indicate which page(s) the two Mindful Moments are on for that week.

Some of the weekly skills or Mindful Moments include physical movements and may need to be modified for children who have physical disabilities or difficulty with motor tasks.

It is important to note that the materials listed in each weekly session are *additional* materials needed. Refer to the following section to determine what materials you will need for every session.

Each Session will need:

- Workbooks for each child

- Pencils

- Crayons and/or colored pencils

- Self-scan poster

- Feeling-Breath-Thought-Skill poster

- Agreements, visual schedule, and family resources based on your setting

Certain Sessions May Need:

- Feelings brainstorm list

- Blank agreements poster

- Measuring challenges poster

- The Triangle poster

- A stuffed animal or lightweight object for each child (Session 4)

- Post-group survey

- Music

- Bean bag or ball to toss around

- Balloons (be aware of latex allergies)

- Marker

Naming Our Feelings

Outline

o Opening practice, create agreements & visual schedule

o Mindful Moment & Feelings Check: *Slow Deep Belly Breaths* (p. 113)

o Activity: Feeling Scenarios & Body Outline

o Weekly Skills: Flying Bird, Smell the Flower & Frog Mouth

o Mindful Moment & Feelings Check: *Breathe in Relaxation* (p. 114)

o Closing Practice & Family Resource

Additional Materials

☐ Bean bag or ball to toss around (optional)

☐ Feelings brainstorm list with marker

☐ Blank agreements poster

Introduction

*Begin by greeting the children and telling them how excited you are to have them here today. Start with your **opening practice,** and then co-create the **group agreements.** Next, review your **visual schedule.***

Mindful Moment & Feelings Check

We are going to be working together over the next twelve weeks to learn about many different ways to relax. We will be practicing a lot, and you are going to get really good at learning to calm down your brain and body. If it's hard at first, that's okay! Doing hard things and making mistakes are how we learn and grow! The first thing we are going to practice today is called a Mindful Moment. If you've never done something like this before, it might feel a little weird or uncomfortable or even silly, or it might feel really calm, peaceful, and relaxing! All feelings are accepted here. During the Mindful Moment, I will be reading you some words. You will listen and follow along.

Before we start our first Mindful Moment, I want you to do a self-scan. A self-scan is when you look at your body and make sure your body is doing what you want it to do. *Review the* **self-scan poster**. During the Mindful Moment, I want you to try to have a calm and quiet body and mouth, just for a minute or two, and then we'll have a chance to talk again! What do you think it means to have a quiet mouth? *Wait for responses.* Not talking or making noises—yes, great! When we do a Mindful Moment, my voice will be the only one you hear. Now, what does it mean to have a quiet body? Is this a quiet body? *Show an example of a very active, moving body.* No? Okay, what does a quiet body look like, then? Can you show me? *Wait a moment.* Great! A quiet body means you are not moving your body. So, do a self-scan right now and make sure you have a quiet body and mouth before we get started on our first Mindful Moment. I know it can be hard to keep your body and mouth quiet, but it will just be for a minute or two, and then we will talk.

Read the **Slow Deep Belly Breaths Mindful Moment** (page 113) script. Be sure to pause between lines and model taking deep breaths. After the Mindful Moment, you will do a **Feelings Check**. Pass an object around the room, such as a bean bag or ball, and have the kids take turns sharing briefly how they feel right now, in the present moment. Model this for them first. Be sure to emphasize that there are no bad or wrong feelings.

Activity

Feelings Scenarios and Body Outline

Together, we will be learning skills to handle our big feelings, like when we feel stressed, mad, sad, nervous, anxious, or worried. One of the skills we are going to work on this week is being able to name our feelings. Let's brainstorm the names of some feelings together, and I will write down a big list of as many different feeling words that we can come up with. *Write down a list of various feeling words on the* **Feelings Brainstorm List**. *Consider hanging this up for future sessions so the children can refer to it during the Feelings Check.*

Okay, great! Guess what? I am an adult, and I have ALL of these feelings sometimes! Feelings are okay! There are no bad or wrong feelings! Some feelings might make me a little uncomfortable, but that's okay; they won't last forever.

Feelings come and feelings go. They are like visitors that stay for a while and leave until a different one comes along. When I have a big feeling, I can name it like this: "I am feeling angry and disappointed" or "I am feeling super sad" or "I am feeling jealous." If I have a big feeling, I will say what it is, and that will help me understand it and make a choice on what to do with it. When we name our feelings, it helps us gain control over them.

Now, let's practice naming our feelings. I am going to give you a situation, and you will tell me how you would feel in that situation. Try to use some of the feeling words we just wrote down. Ready? *You can throw a bean bag or pass a ball for each person's turn to review the feelings situations or simply call on each child. Feel free to do this as frequently or infrequently as time permits!*

Feelings Situations

- You fall down at recess

- You get invited to a pool party

- Someone cuts you in line

- You forget your Valentines at home

- Your friend says you can't play with them

- You get blamed for something you didn't do

- You have a big test coming up

- A hornet lands on your shirt

- You win a free trip to Disney World for you and your family

- Your teacher asks you to move because you were talking

What do you think it means to be stressed, nervous, anxious, or worried? What does it look like when you feel like this? What is it like inside your body when you have big feelings? *Share an example of a less-obvious sign your body experiences when stressed such as clenching your teeth when nervous.*

I am going to pass out your workbooks. I want you to write your name on the cover. *Pause.* Now you are going to use your crayons or colored pencils to fill in the **Body Outline** in your workbook to show how it feels inside your body when you have these big feelings. Be creative—there is no right or wrong way to do this. Every person's body is different, so we all experience stress differently, too. Is it okay to make mistakes in your art? Yes! Some of the greatest artists have experimented with their mistakes to create even better and more interesting art.

Give the children some time to color, and then give them a transition warning (e.g., I want you to know you have two minutes left to color, so please find a good stopping point. Remember, if you don't finish it now, you can work on this later.). Wait about 1.5 minutes and offer another transition warning (e.g., Okay you have about 30 seconds left, so please find a place where you can stop coloring and close your coloring workbook. I know it can be hard to pause, but we have more fun activities to do!) Refer to the visual schedule as needed.

- o   Flying Bird
- o   Smell the Flower
- o   Frog Mouth

Weekly Skills

This week, I am so excited to teach you the three weekly skills! The first skill is called **Flying Bird**. This is a really great calming skill! I want you to watch me, and then we'll practice together. Cross your arms on your chest with your fingers pointed up towards your neck. Interlock your thumbs. Take some slow, deep belly breaths while you tap your hands, or wings, in a pattern one and then the other. Great!

The second skill of the week is called **Smell the Flower**. Imagine you are holding a flower and breathe in through your nose to smell the wonderful scent. Next, pretend you are blowing out a candle by blowing air out through tight lips. Whenever you are practicing deep breaths, you always want to make sure your out-breath, or your exhale, is longer than your in-breath, or inhale. If you feel yourself getting a little dizzy, it means that you need to make your out-breath longer.

Before we do the last skill for the week, I need to tell you something really important. Whenever we are learning skills or doing stretches, I want you to make sure that you do what feels good and comfortable for your own body. Listen to your body, and don't overdo it. If something hurts, then please stop. You only want to do what feels good for you, and we are all different and unique.

The last skill for this week is called **Frog Mouth**. It's kind of a silly one! Pretend you are a frog and open your mouth as wide as you can to stretch your jaw wide open. Hold the stretch for ten seconds. Now, relax and release your mouth as much as you can and use your hands to massage your jaw on both sides. Do you feel the difference between the tense and the loose sensations?

Now, I am going to give you some time to color in your three skills! You can color these any way you want. There are no right or wrong ways! This is your special workbook, so, if you want a rainbow polka-dotted frog, that's great! Be creative.

While the children are coloring, ask them questions (e.g., "When do you think it would be a good time to use these skills?"). Many children have trouble sleeping, so you can encourage them to practice their skills before bedtime. Remember to watch the time and give the children a transition warning before they need to stop coloring. Refer back to the visual schedule as needed.

We are wrapping up for today. We are going to end with the **Breathe in Relaxation Mindful Moment** (page 114) and then do our **Feelings Check**. *Refer to the visual schedule. Emphasize the importance of paying attention to their feelings in the present moment during the Feelings Check.*

This week, I want you to practice your three skills and naming your feelings. Try to practice a little bit every day if you can. An important part of these sessions is practicing the skills you learn throughout the week. Make a plan with your families about where and when you will practice. It would be great if you could practice together! *End with your **Closing Practice** and hand out the weekly **Family Resource,** if it applies to your setting.*

FAMILY RESOURCE 1

Naming Our Feelings

This week, we learned about the importance of naming our feelings. We also identified what it feels like in our bodies to have big feelings like stress, anger, sadness, anxiety, or worry. Most children experience a full range of emotions, but they do not yet have the emotional vocabularies to describe all the feelings that they experience beyond the basic terms like sad and mad. We started our first session by talking about what some of the big feeling words mean, such as stressed, angry, and worried. Here are some activities you can do at home to work on expanding your child's emotional vocabulary:

- Write down a big list of feeling words together.

- Make a face and body posture that matches each feeling.

- Create a noise to match each feeling.

- Create "emotional thermometers" for different feeling states and discuss what would make the "temperature" of a feeling change (e.g., from fine to a little annoyed to disappointed to frustrated to mad to angry to furious to enraged).

- When reading books or watching a movie, pause and ask what your child thinks certain characters are feeling and why they may be feeling that way. Discuss how body language and facial expressions give you clues to other people's feelings.

- Play emotions charades (i.e., take turns acting out a feeling nonverbally and guessing the feeling).

- Talk about your own feelings in an appropriate manner. Remember some topics may not be appropriate for children, so be sure to use good boundaries when practicing this.

There is power in being able to name and acknowledge your feelings. In the book, *The Whole-Brain Child: 12 Revolutionary Strategies to Nurture Your Child's Developing Mind*[1], Siegel and Payne Bryson write about the importance of identifying feelings and how we can "name it to tame it." When we engage the left side of our brain in thinking about the right word to describe our feelings, this can help diffuse our big feelings. Naming our feelings can also help us own them, which can help lessen their power over us.

You can model this by using your words to name and express feelings appropriately. It is helpful for our children to see us doing this in our day to day lives. They need to see you using your words and naming how you feel, too. Here are some examples of this:

- "I am feeling frustrated because your room is a mess."

- "I am feeling anxious because I have this big work deadline soon."

- "I am feeling irritated with your tone of voice."

- "I am so proud of how hard you worked on this project."

Accepting All Feelings

Once children understand that they need to name and acknowledge their feelings, they must next understand and believe that all feelings are acceptable. Some children may think there are good and bad or positive and negative feelings. They might try to resist acknowledging their "bad" feelings. This is not helpful. The famous psychologist Carl Jung[2] said that "what you resist not only persists, but will grow in size." It is important for your children to realize that every single person—even counselors, family members, and teachers—has all different feelings all the time. Some feelings might make us more comfortable, and others uncomfortable, but there are no wrong or bad feelings. Feelings will come and go, like visitors. We want to emphasize that each child has choices they can make, even when they have big feelings.

---

[1] Siegel, D. J., and Payne Bryson, T. (2011). *The whole-brain child: 12 revolutionary strategies to nurture your child's developing mind.* Random House.

[2] Jung, C. (n.d.), as cited in Seltzer, L. F. (2016, June 15). You only get more of what you resist-why? *Psychology Today.* https://www.psychologytoday.com/us/blog/evolution-the-self/201606/you-only-get more-what-you-resist-why

Skills to Practice This Week

Each week, your child is going to learn three new skills to practice at home. Make this an opportunity to connect and practice together! The skills are fun and very brief, so they won't take more than a couple of minutes to do. Work with your child to figure out a time and place where you can make practicing the skills part of your daily routine. Some examples could be before bedtime in the child's room, after teeth brushing in the kitchen, or before homework in the living room. Don't make practicing the skills stressful or turn it into a struggle. The reason we encourage the children to practice the skills during the week when they are feeling calm is that the more often they practice the skills, the easier it will be for them to use them when they are having big feelings, as their muscle memory will kick in.

Flying Bird

Cross your arms on your chest with your fingers pointed up towards your neck. Interlock your thumbs. Take some slow, deep belly breaths while you tap your hands, or wings, in a pattern — one and then the other.

Smell the Flower

Imagine you are holding a flower and breathe in through your nose to smell the wonderful scent. Next, pretend you are blowing out a candle by blowing air out through tight lips.

Frog Mouth

Pretend you are a frog and open your mouth as wide as you can to stretch your jaw wide open. Hold the stretch for ten seconds. Now, relax and release your mouth as much as you can and use your hands to massage your jaw on both sides. Do you feel the difference between the tense and the loose sensations?

Triggers

Outline

- o Opening practice, agreements & visual schedule

- o Mindful Moment & Feelings Check: *Wave Breath* (p. 115)

- o Activity: Triggers & F-B-T-S

- o Weekly Skills: Sun and Sand, Gorilla Hug & Snowman Stress Melter Breath

- o Mindful Moment & Feelings Check: *Body Scan* (p. 116)

- o Closing Practice & Family Resource

Additional Materials

- ☐ Bean bag or ball

Introduction

*Start with your **opening practice.** Remember the opening and closing practices can be very brief, but they should remain the same at each session. Review the group **agreements** you made last week, and then review your **visual schedule**.*

Mindful Moment & Feelings Check

*Review the self-scan visual. Read the **Wave Breath Mindful Moment** (page 115) and, afterward, do a brief **Feelings Check,** which you will model for them first.*

Last week, we learned that there are no bad or wrong feelings. For our check-in today, I want you to notice how you are feeling right now, in this room, in this very moment. When we pay attention to the present moment, it is called being mindful, and it's something we'll learn more about and practice together. When we check-in with our feelings, you may also want to share if you practiced naming your feelings over the past week and how that went for you.

Triggers and F-B-T-S

Activity

This week, we are going to talk about things that make us feel stressed, mad, sad, nervous, anxious, or worried. A thing that usually makes you feel upset is called a "trigger." Not getting enough sleep or moving enough, being hungry, or using too much technology can be triggers for a lot of us. *Share an example of one of your own triggers, such as when there is too much traffic when you're already late.*

It's good to know your triggers, because, if you know that a certain thing is usually hard for you, you can plan to use a skill to cope with it better. Let's pretend that school assemblies are very loud and that loud noises usually cause you to feel overwhelmed. If you know loud assemblies are a trigger, you can plan to bring your noise-canceling headphones and practice a skill beforehand, like Smell the Flower. Now, let's turn to the trigger worksheet in your workbook. We will do this together. Put your finger on number one. I will read it and I want you to circle it if it is a trigger for you—a thing that bothers you a lot. If it doesn't bother you too much and is not a trigger, then cross it out. Remember that there are no right or wrong answers to this. We will all have different answers and that's okay! *After going through the activity, you can ask them to put a check next to their top three triggers. If time allows, children may want to share.*

We can't avoid our triggers, but we can practice getting good at coping with them! One of the strategies that we are going to practice is called Feeling-Breath-Thought-Skill, or F-B-T-S for short. It's great to use when you have big feelings or when you know a trigger will be happening. *Review the **Feeling-Breath-Thought-Skill poster.***

- Name your **Feelings**: "I am feeling _____."

- Take three slow, deep **Breaths**.

- Choose helpful, happy **Thoughts**, such as telling yourself, "This is just a feeling. It will pass. I will be okay."

- Pick a **Skill** to practice: "I choose _____."

To help the children learn and remember the strategy, you can toss around a bean bag or ball and do the F-B-T-S chant with each throw. Repeating one letter and then one word with each toss: "F – B – T – S – Feeling – Breath - Thought – Skill-F-B-T-S-Feeling-Breath-Thought-Skill." Try to work together, repeating the chant while getting progressively quicker.

- ○ Sun and Sand
- ○ Gorilla Hug
- ○ Snowman Stress Melter Breath

Weekly Skills

Now, we are going to switch gears and learn our three weekly skills! Our first skill this week is called **Sun and Sand.** Watch me and then we will do it together. Envision that you are at the beach on a beautiful summer day. Sit criss-cross apple-sauce on the sand. Breathe in and stretch your arms up high above your head, reaching towards the sun and lengthening your body. Feel your shoulders stretch. Now, breathe out and reach your arms out in front of you towards the sand. Hold the stretch for ten seconds and relax here.

Our second skill this week is called **Gorilla Hug**. Watch me, and then we'll do it together. Wrap your arms around your torso and give yourself a big, giant gorilla hug. Squeeze if it feels comfortable. Uncross your arms and try again with the opposite arm on top. Uncross your arms and now try giving yourself a big giant gorilla hug over your shoulders. Now try again with the opposite arm on top.

Our last skill this week is a favorite! This is a skill you can practice on paper with a pencil or crayon, or you can trace it in the palm of your hand. It's called **Snowman Stress Melter Breath**. Watch me do it, and then we'll practice together. Place your pointer finger on the bow tie and follow the arrows as you trace your finger around the snowman's head, breathing in. When you come back to the bowtie, start to breathe out a very long and slow breath and trace your finger around the snowman's body. Repeat and feel your stress melt away.

At this point, I like to have each child put their workbook in front of them and watch them practice the Snowman Stress Melter Breath to make sure they understand when to breathe in and out while tracing. If time allows, you can also review the three skills from the previous week. I like to call out the names of skills and have the children practice them. Alternatively, you can also go around in a circle and ask each child to name a skill and then the group can practice it together, or a child can demonstrate a skill to the group and the group can name it.

Next, give the children time to color the three new skills in their workbooks. Remember to provide them with a transition warning before moving on and refer back to the visual schedule, as needed.

Wrap Up

We are wrapping up for today. We are going to end with a **Body Scan Mindful Moment** (page 116) and then do our **Feelings Check**. *Refer to the visual schedule. Emphasize the importance of paying attention to their feelings in the present moment.*

This week you can continue practicing naming your feelings and after you say how you feel, you can take three deep breaths. These are the first two steps in F-B-T-S! You can also try to notice your triggers over the week and practice your three weekly skills.

*End with your **Closing Practice** and hand out the weekly **Family Resource,** if it applies to your setting.*

Triggers, Sleep, and Nutrition

This week, we learned about triggers. Being hungry, using too much technology, or not getting enough sleep or physical activity can be triggers for many of us. Since everyone is unique, we all have different triggers. It's important to know what our triggers are so we can be prepared to practice our skills. We can't avoid our triggers, but we can learn to cope with them more effectively.

You can help your child with their overall wellness by ensuring that they are getting enough sleep, eating a healthy diet, limiting and monitoring their media usage, and increasing their physical activity. This session, we will focus on nutrition and sleep, but we will talk more about some of these issues in future sessions.

Research on the ties between diet and mental health in children and adolescents notes that there are "significant relationships between unhealthy dietary patterns and poorer mental health." [3] Encourage your children to stay hydrated and eat a well-balanced diet, limiting caffeine and sugary foods/beverages.

Getting enough sleep is extremely impactful for children's development. The American Academy of Sleep Medicine (AASM) recommends that children six to twelve years old get nine to twelve hours of sleep each night. They report that getting enough sleep regularly contributes to "improved attention, behavior, learning, memory, emotional regulation, quality of life, and mental and physical health." [4] The American Academy of Pediatrics (AAP) recommends turn-

---

[3] O'Neil, A., Quirk, S. E, Housden, S., Brennan, S. L, Williams, L. J, Pasco, J. A, Berk, M. & Jacka, F. N. (2014). Relationship between diet and mental health in children and adolescents: a systematic review. *American Journal of Public Health, (104)*10, e31-e42. https://www.doi.org/10.2105/AJPH.2014.302110

[4] Paruthi, S., Brooks, L. J., D'Ambrosio, C., Hall, W. A., Kotagal, S., Lloyd, R. M., Malow, B. A., Maski, K., Nichols, C., Quan, S. F., Rosen, C. L., Troester, M. M., & Wise, M. S. (2016). Recommended amount of sleep for pediatric populations: A consensus statement of the American Academy of Sleep Medicine. *Journal of clinical sleep medicine: official publication of the American Academy of Sleep Medicine, 12*(6), 785–786. https://www.doi.org/10.5664/jcsm.5866

ing off screens 30 minutes before bedtime. [5] They have published a free online resource on bedtime routines called "Brush, Book, Bath." [6]

---

[5] American Academy of Pediatrics (2016, June 13). *American academy of pediatrics supports childhood sleep guidelines.* American Academy of Pediatrics.
https://www.healthychildren.org/English/news/Pages/AAP-Supports-Childhood-Sleep-Guidelines.aspx

[6] American Academy of Pediatrics (2014, June 7). *Brush, book, bed: how to structure your child's nighttime routine.* Healthy Children. http://bit.ly/bedroutine

Skills to Practice This Week

Continue to practice the skills from last week while adding in these three new skills:

Sun and Sand

Envision you are at the beach on a beautiful summer day. Sit criss-cross applesauce on the sand. Breathe in and stretch your arms up high above your head, reaching towards the sun and lengthening your body. Feel your shoulders stretch. Now, breathe out and reach your arms out in front of you towards the sand. Hold the stretch for ten seconds and relax here.

Gorilla Hug

Wrap your arms around your torso and give yourself a big, giant gorilla hug. Squeeze if it feels comfortable. Uncross your arms and try again with the opposite arm on top. Uncross your arms and now try giving yourself a big, giant gorilla hug over your shoulders. Now try again with the opposite arm on top.

Snowman Stress Melter Breath

Place your pointer finger on the bow tie and follow the arrows as you trace your finger around the snowman's head while you breathe in. When you come back to the bow tie, start to breathe out a very long and slow breath as you trace your finger around the snowman's body. Repeat and feel your stress melt away.

Helpful and Unhelpful Thoughts

Outline

o Opening practice, agreements & visual schedule

o Mindful Moment & Feelings Check: *Happy Helpful Message* (p. 117)

o Activity: Helpful and Unhelpful Thoughts

o Weekly Skills: Snail Shell, Flat Tire & Helpful, Happy Thoughts

o Mindful Moment & Feelings Check: *Muscle Relaxation* (p. 118)

o Closing Practice & Family Resource

Additional Materials

☐ The Triangle poster

Introduction

Start the session with your **opening practice.** *Remember, the opening and closing practices should remain the same each session. Review your* **group agreements** *and your* **visual schedule.**

Mindful Moment & Feelings Check

Have the children do a self-scan and use the visual, as needed. Then read the **Happy Helpful Message Mindful Moment** *(page 117). Next, do a* **Feelings Check,** *during which you can also do a brief review of the previous week:* Last week, we learned about triggers. As we do our feelings check, if you want to, you can share whether or not you noticed any triggers over the past week and if you practiced naming your feelings and taking three deep breaths, which are the first two steps in F-B-T-S.

Helpful and Unhelpful Thoughts

Activity

This week, we are going to learn about thoughts. *Show the **Triangle poster**.* Thoughts are words or pictures you imagine in your brain. Your thoughts control how you feel, which impacts how you act. So, if you can change your thoughts, you can change your mood and even your actions!

Helpful thoughts make you feel good and unhelpful thoughts make you feel lousy. Let's try an example: If I am thinking, "What? There's no more yogurt? I HATE Mondays! Today is going to be terrible!" How am I going to feel? How am I going to act? Now, what if I said to myself, "I feel disappointed there is no more yogurt left for breakfast today, but I will take three deep breaths to make the best out of it. I am going to have a good day anyway. I know it is Monday, but at least I have gym today! I will practice Sun and Sand." Now how am I going to feel? How will I act?

Let's practice this together! Please turn to the **Helpful and Unhelpful Thoughts** page in your workbook. Put an X next to the unhelpful thoughts and circle the helpful thoughts. *Work on Helpful and Unhelpful Thoughts page together.*

This week, I want you to be a detective and pay attention to both your helpful and unhelpful thoughts. Just because you think a certain thought, does it mean it is 100 percent true? No! If I think, "I am dumb," is that true? No way! That is an unhelpful thought that will make me feel lousy though! Let's review our F-B-T-S strategy now. *Take out the **F-B-T-S poster** and ask the children if they remember what each letter stands for. Next, practice the "F-B-T-S-Feeling-Breath-Thought-Skill" chant a few times together.*

Weekly Skills

Our first skill is called **Snail Shell**. Imagine you are a snail in a lovely garden with beautiful flowers all around. Take a break from the garden by hiding inside your snail shell. Gently push your head down to hide inside your shell as you lift your shoulders up towards your head. Hold this position for ten seconds. Now, take a big breath in and stretch out of your shell by lifting your head and heart up high and pulling your shoulders back down as you breathe out.

- ○ Snail Shell
- ○ Flat Tire
- ○ Helpful, Happy Thoughts

53

Our second skill is called **Flat Tire**. Breathe in while flexing your arms up above your head to make a tire shape. Now, breathe out while very gently and slowly lowering your arms and making a "shhh" sound. All the air drains out of the tire, just as all of the stress flows out of your body.

Our last skill is called **Helpful, Happy Thoughts**. When you think helpful, happy thoughts, you will feel comfortable. When you think unhelpful thoughts, you will feel uncomfortable. What do you like to think about? Are there certain people? Things? Animals? Places? Games? Colors? Sounds? Music? Memories? If you want to, close your eyes for a minute and think of some of your helpful, happy thoughts.

Give the children time to illustrate or write down some of their helpful, happy thoughts in their workbook on the Helpful, Happy Thoughts page and to color their three weekly skills. Remember to use the visual schedule and give transition warnings before they need to stop coloring and move on.

Wrap Up

We are wrapping up for today. We are going to end with a **Muscle Relaxation Mindful Moment** (page 118) and then do our **Feelings Check**. *Refer to the visual schedule as needed.*

This week, I want you to practice paying attention to your thoughts! Just notice if you have unhelpful or helpful thoughts. If you have unhelpful thoughts, don't get upset or judge yourself. We all have unhelpful thoughts sometimes! I want you to practice noticing and being aware of your thoughts. You can also continue to practice F-B-T-S!

*End with your **closing practice** and hand out the weekly **Family Resource**, if it applies to your setting.*

Helpful and Unhelpful Thoughts

Our lesson this week was on how your thoughts affect your feelings, which impacts your behavior, and how your behavior then reinforces your thoughts. So, when you change your thoughts, you interrupt this cycle and can change your feelings. Understanding and applying this concept can be helpful for everyone, including children.

You can help your child be a detective to figure out what they are thinking. Just because they think a certain thought, does it mean it is 100 percent true? Practice making up helpful and unhelpful thoughts and identifying them. Many of us have inaccurate or unhelpful thoughts. It is important that your child does not start to believe that their unhelpful thoughts are true.

Our brains don't know how to distinguish between when we are just thinking a thought and when it is actually happening. This means that if your child has an unhelpful thought (e.g., "What if a meteor crashes into my house?"), their body will engage in a cascade of effects that will physiologically increase arousal, tension, and stress. When your child changes their thoughts to a more helpful thought, they can change their feelings and bodily responses as well. Children can learn that they have the power to control their own thoughts!

Most children will need reminders that there are differences between feelings, thoughts, and behaviors. You can remind them that they will have many different feelings and that it is okay. Feelings will come and go. Some feelings are uncomfortable, but children can still healthily express their feelings and make positive choices.

Big Takeaways:

- Your thoughts control how you feel and your feelings impact your behavior.

- Not all of your thoughts are true or accurate.

- Helpful thoughts make you feel comfortable, and unhelpful thoughts make you feel uncomfortable.

- If you change your thoughts, you can change how you are feeling.

Skills to Practice This Week

Snail Shell

Imagine you are a snail in a lovely garden with beautiful flowers all around. Take a break from the garden by hiding inside your snail shell. Gently push your head down to hide inside your shell as you lift your shoulders up towards your head. Hold this position for ten seconds. Now take a big breath in and stretch out of your shell by lifting your head and heart up high and pulling your shoulders back down as you breathe out.

Flat Tire

Breathe in while flexing your arms up above your head to make a tire shape. Now, breathe out while very gently and slowly lowering your arms and making a "shhh" sound. All the air drains out of the tire, just as all the stress flows out of your body.

Helpful, Happy Thoughts

Think about helpful, happy things that you like, whether they're memories, games, animals, places, music, or people. If you are comfortable, close your eyes for a minute and think of your helpful, happy thoughts.

Changing Thoughts

Outline

- o Opening practice, agreements & visual schedule

- o Mindful Moment & Feelings Check: *Elephant Ears* (p. 119)

- o Activity: Thought Changer

- o Weekly Skills: Fly Away, Ladybug, Buddy Breath & Elephant Ears

- o Mindful Moment & Feelings Check: *Gentle Body Movements* (p. 120)

- o Closing Practice & Family Resource

Additional Materials

- ☐ A stuffed animal or lightweight object for each child

- ☐ The Triangle poster

Introduction

*Start with your **opening practice**. Next, review your **group agreements** and your **visual schedule**.*

Mindful Moment & Feelings Check

*Ask the children to do a self-scan. Use a visual if needed. Then read the **Elephant Ears Mindful Moment** (page 119). Next, do a **Feelings Check**, during which you can also do a brief review of the previous week:* Last week, we learned about helpful and unhelpful thoughts. *Review the **Triangle poster**.* Does anyone want to share anything they noticed over the past week when they were a detective? Did you catch yourself thinking both helpful and unhelpful thoughts? How were you feeling? What did you do? *Share an appropriate example from your week. If children share unhelpful thoughts, have them practice working together to turn them into more helpful thoughts.*

Activity

Thought Changer

This week, we're going to practice changing some unhelpful thoughts into more helpful thoughts! Turn to the **Thought Changer** page in your workbook and we'll do this activity together. *Review the **F-B-T-S** Poster. Use some of the Thought Changer scenarios to practice using F-B-T-S. If your group is limited on time, consider discussing each thought on the Thought Changer worksheet instead of having the children write down new thoughts.*

If you start to have big feelings, check-in with yourself to see what type of thoughts you are having. Be a detective. Once you are aware of your thoughts, you can begin to change them. Your feelings and body sensations can give you clues too! Some types of unhelpful thoughts include the following:

⇨ "What if" thoughts, like "What if something terrible happens today?"

⇨ Extreme black-or-white thinking, such as when you use words like "never" or "always." Examples of this would be thinking, "I NEVER get what I want!" or "I ALWAYS lose at soccer!"

⇨ Using words like "should," "must," or "ought," which make us feel bad about ourselves or others. An example of this would be thinking, "I SHOULD have known better!"

Weekly Skills

Our first skill today is called **Fly Away, Ladybug**. It's a stretch for your face and it's a really silly one to start with! Imagine a lucky ladybug landed on your nose and is tickling you. You don't want to use your hands to touch her, but you want her to fly away home. So, pucker up your face really tight. Squeeze your nose and eyes. Feel all the wrinkles and stiffness in your forehead, cheeks, mouth, and eyes. Hold this position for ten seconds. Now, relax and loosen all of your face muscles so they melt and soften again.

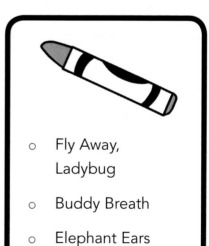

- ○ Fly Away, Ladybug
- ○ Buddy Breath
- ○ Elephant Ears

Pass out an object, such as a stuffed animal, to each child in preparation for Buddy Breath. If you don't have enough stuffed animals, feel free to use another lightweight object. If you are in a whole classroom setting, you might have to be creative with how to do this one as it requires enough space for everyone to lie down! In a large class without space for everyone to lie down, I have had the children lean back slightly and place their hand on their belly instead of an object.

Our next skill is called **Buddy Breath**. We need to lay down for this one, as long as you are comfortable. You also need a stuffed buddy *(alter script according to the object you intend to use)*. After you lie down, place your buddy on your belly *(alter script according to the position you ask the children to get into for the skill)*. Take a slow, deep breath in, filling your belly up with air, and watch your buddy lift up and rise. Now, breathe out very slowly and watch your buddy slowly fall. Repeat with slow, deep breaths in and out as you watch your buddy rise and fall gently with the rhythm of your breath.

Our last skill for today is called **Elephant Ears** and it's a really nice simple way to take care of yourself. Take your thumbs and pointer fingers and place them on your ear lobes. Pull down gently and lightly massage, starting at the bottom of your ear lobe and working your way up to the top of your ear.

Give the children time to color their three weekly skills. Remember to provide them with transition warnings and use the visual schedule before moving on.

Wrap Up

We are wrapping up for today. We are going to end with a **Gentle Body Movements Mindful Moment** (page 120) and then do our **Feelings Check**. *Refer to the visual schedule.* This week, you will continue to be a detective and you will practice F-B-T-S! *End with your closing practice and hand out the weekly **Family Resource**, if it applies to your setting.*

Feeling-Breath-Thought-Skill

This week, we practiced changing unhelpful thoughts into helpful thoughts and using the strategy called Feeling-Breath-Thought-Skill (F-B-T-S.)

F = Name your **feeling**. "I am feeling _____."

B = Take three slow, deep **breaths**.

T = Choose helpful, happy **thoughts**. "This is just a feeling. It will pass. I will be okay."

S = Pick a **skill** to practice. "I choose _____."

Modeling

It is important to model emotional regulation and using healthy coping skills for your children. Children are like sponges, and the old-fashioned "do as I say, not as I do" mentality just doesn't work. We can tell a child to do something, but they are more likely to do it when they see us doing it ourselves. So, if you over-react to something or make a mistake, acknowledge it to your child and apologize for it. Model the behavior you wish to see in your children.

You can narrate your thoughts aloud to teach your children the F-B-T-S process. For example, you might say, "Oh no! My coffee just spilled all over my new jacket! I am feeling embarrassed and angry with myself!" and take three deep breaths to calm yourself. Then model helpful, happy thoughts such as the fact your jacket wasn't white and the coffee probably won't stain. Finally, choose a skill to curb your big feelings, such as Snowman Stress Melter Breath.

Skills to Practice This Week

Fly Away, Ladybug

Imagine a lucky ladybug landed on your nose and is tickling you. You don't want to use your hands to touch her, but you want her to fly away home. So, pucker up your face really tight. Squeeze your nose and eyes. Feel all the wrinkles and stiffness in your forehead, cheeks, mouth, and eyes. Hold this position for ten seconds. Now, relax and loosen all of your face muscles so they melt and soften again.

Buddy Breath

Lie down and place an object, such as a stuffed animal, on your belly. Take a slow, deep breath in, filling your belly up with air, and watch the object rise. Now, breathe out very slowly and watch the object slowly fall with your belly. Repeat a few more slow, deep breaths in and out as you watch the object rise and fall gently with the rhythm of your breath.

Elephant Ears

Take your thumbs and pointer fingers and place them on your ear lobes. Pull down gently and lightly massage, starting at the bottom of your ear lobe and working your way up to the top of your ear.

Measuring Challenges

Outline

o Opening practice, agreements & visual schedule

o Mindful Moment & Feelings Check: *Rainbow Walk* (p. 122)

o Activity: *Measuring Challenges*

o Weekly Skills: *Measuring Challenges, Ski Jumper & Balloon Breath*

o Mindful Moment & Feelings Check: *Breathe in Relaxation* (p. 114)

o Closing Practice & Family Resource

Additional Materials

☐ Measuring Challenges poster

☐ The Triangle poster

Introduction

*Start with your **opening practice.** Next, review your **group agreements** and your **visual schedule.***

Mindful Moment & Feelings Check

*Ask the children to do a self-scan. Use a visual if needed. Then read the **Rainbow Walk Mindful Moment** (page 122) followed by a **Feelings Check**, during which you can also do a review of the previous week:* Last week, we learned how to change unhelpful thoughts into helpful thoughts. *Review the **Triangle Poster**.* Were you able to change any unhelpful thoughts into helpful thoughts? Does anyone want to share how they were able to change their thoughts? Did you practice the Feeling-Breath-Thought-Skill strategy this week? How did it go for you?

Measuring Challenges

Activity

This week, we will learn about measuring challenges. In life, we all have challenges, obstacles, or problems sometimes. An obstacle is something that gets in the way of your progress. It might make things harder for you or it might block you from reaching your goals or getting where you are trying to go. Some of these may be tiny challenges and others may be huge obstacles. Today, we are going to learn about measuring our challenges. This is our scale: *show **Measuring Challenges poster**.*

The first type of challenge is a small rock challenge and it's barely even a problem because it doesn't bother you too much. You don't even really consider it an obstacle or problem, so you have no reaction or a very tiny one. An example of a small rock problem would be a pebble in your shoe, so you pause and dump the pebble out, or a broken pencil, so you just sharpen your pencil or get a new one. Since you solve these small rock challenges quickly, you feel fine about them, and you don't spend too much time thinking about them.

The next type of challenge is a medium boulder challenge. You can solve this challenge yourself by using some of your strategies. An example would be someone sitting next to you and tapping their pencil on your desk. This is an annoying obstacle, but it's solved easily by asking the person to stop tapping the pencil or moving away from them. Other strategies used to solve medium boulder challenges could be talking the problem out, ignoring something, walking away from the problem, sharing with someone, or thinking helpful, happy thoughts. You might feel annoyed with a medium boulder challenge, but you can handle it!

The next type of challenge is called a big hill challenge. You usually need some help from someone to solve this kind of challenge and it might impact several people and take a while to solve. An example of a big hill challenge would be getting into an argument with someone who yells at you to "mind your own business" and then throws their yogurt at you and ruins your new shirt. You would be feeling pretty upset or bothered! Some strategies to solve big hill challenges include asking for help, apologizing, or making a compromise.

The last challenge type is called a huge volcano challenge. This takes longer to solve because there is not a quick and easy solution. It may impact a lot of people and you have lots of big feelings about it. You might feel furious, enraged, panicked, or terrified. It may even be an unsafe or dangerous situation, like an emergency, so the strategies for solving the challenge may be big, like calling 9-1-1, running away, or yelling for an adult's help. An example of a huge volcano challenge would be getting hurt in a very bad car accident, or experiencing a kitchen fire at your aunt's house, or a volcano erupting while you're on vacation.

Now, let's practice our **Measuring Challenges** scenarios in your workbook. I am going to read you a challenge and when it's your turn, you will tell us what type of challenge you think it is.

Review the **F-B-T-S poster** *and incorporate Measuring Challenges into the helpful, happy thoughts this week:*

- Name your **feeling**: "I am feeling _____."

- Take three slow, deep **breaths.**

- Choose happy, helpful **thoughts**. "This is just a feeling. It will pass. I will be okay. This is a big hill challenge. I can ask for help!"

- Pick a **skill** to practice. "I choose _____."

Weekly Skills

The first skill this week is about **Measuring Challenges**. If you have a challenge, take three deep breaths and ask yourself, "How big is this challenge? Is my response equal to the challenge? If not, which skills will I use to cool down?"

Our second skill this week is **Ski Jumper**. Raise both of your arms up above your head and then swing them back behind you as you bend slightly forward at the waist while keeping your back straight. Now, continue to swing your arms as you rock forward and backward and feel the air rushing by your

- Measuring Challenges
- Ski Jumper
- Balloon Breath

arms. When you lean forward, your arms swing back, and, when you lean back, your arms swing forward.

Our last skill this week is called **Balloon Breath**. This one is fun and it kind of tickles your lips. First, interlace your fingers and place them on your belly. Imagine you are using your breath to inflate a balloon in front of your belly. What color is your balloon? Breathe in and slowly lift your arms out in front of you as the balloon blows up. Now, breathe out through your mouth to make a "pfft" raspberry blowing sound with your lips as you slowly lower your arms back down, making the balloon deflate.

Give the children time to color the three skills. Remember to provide them with transition warnings and use the visual schedule before wrapping up and moving on.

Wrap Up

We are wrapping up for today. We are going to end with a **Breathe in Relaxation Mindful Moment** (page 114) and then do our **Feelings Check**. *Refer to the visual schedule.* This week, when you are faced with a challenge, ask yourself what type of challenge it is. You will continue to be a detective, practice your weekly skills, and F-B-T-S.

*End with your **closing practice** and hand out the weekly **Family Resource,** if it applies to your setting.*

Measuring Challenges

This week, we learned that there are different kinds of challenges, obstacles, or problems in life and we used a scale to measure them. The first type of challenge in our scale is a small rock challenge and it's barely noticeable. It elicits little to no reaction from you. It's something like a pebble in your shoe or a shirt that fits too tightly. Since you can resolve these small rock challenges quickly, your general mood is unaffected.

The next type of challenge is a medium boulder challenge. Your child can solve this challenge by using some of the strategies they learned in group. An example of a medium boulder challenge would be someone kicking the back of your seat on a plane or in a movie theater. This is an annoying obstacle, but it is solved easily by using strategies such as asking the person to stop or moving away from them. Other strategies could be discussing the issue, ignoring the annoyance, walking away, sharing an object, or using helpful, happy thoughts. You might feel annoyed with a medium boulder challenge, but you can handle it.

The next type of challenge is called a big hill challenge. You usually need some help from someone to solve this kind of challenge and it might impact several people or take a while to solve. An example of a big hill challenge would be running late to work when you have a high-stakes meeting or a verbal or physical altercation. You would be feeling pretty upset or bothered! Some strategies to solve big hill challenges include asking for help, apologizing, or compromising.

The last type of challenge is called a huge volcano challenge. This takes longer to solve because there's no quick and easy solution for it. It may impact a lot of people, and you will likely have strong emotions as a result of it. You might feel furious, enraged, panicked, or terrified. It may be an unsafe or dangerous situation, like an emergency, so strategies you use to resolve the challenge may be big, like calling 9-1-1, running away, or yelling for help. An example of this type of challenge would be if you were injured in a bad car accident or in any situation that you felt was too much to handle physically or emotionally. When challenges come up this week, you can help your child measure the challenge using this scale. You can also make up challenge scenarios together and measure them.

Skills to Practice This Week

Measuring Challenges

If you have a challenge, take three deep breaths and ask yourself how big the challenge is. Is your response equal to the challenge? If not, which skills can you use to cool down?

 Huge Volcano

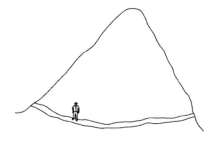 Big Hill

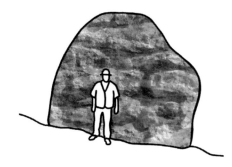 Medium Boulder

 Small Rock

Ski Jumper

Raise both of your arms up above your head and then swing them back behind you as you bend slightly forward at the waist, keeping your back straight. Now, continue to swing your arms as you rock forward and backward and the feel the air rushing by your arms. When you lean forward, your arms swing back, and, when you lean back, your arms swing forward.

Balloon Breath

Interlace your fingers and place them on your belly. Imagine you are using your breath to inflate a balloon in front of your belly. What color is your balloon? Breathe in slowly and lift your arms out in front of you as the balloon blows up. Now, breathe out through your mouth to make a "pfft" raspberry blowing sound with your lips as you slowly lower your arms back down, making the balloon deflate.

Equal Measurements

Outline

- o Opening practice, agreements & visual schedule

- o Mindful Moment & Feelings Check: *Equal Breathing* (p. 123)

- o Activity: Equal Measurements

- o Weekly Skills: Orange Squeeze, Equal Breathing & Hand Massage

- o Mindful Moment & Feelings Check: *Body Scan* (p. 116)

- o Closing Practice & Family Resource

Additional Materials

- ☐ Measuring Challenges poster

Introduction

Start with your **opening practice,** *and then review your group* **agreements** *and your* **visual schedule.**

Mindful Moment & Feelings Check

Ask the children to do a self-scan. Use a visual if needed. Then, read the **Equal Breathing Mindful Moment** *(page 123) followed by a* **Feelings Check,** *during which you can also do a brief review of the previous week:* Last week, we learned about measuring challenges. *Review the* **Measuring Challenges poster.** As we check-in with our feelings this week, you can choose to share what you noticed over the past week when you measured your challenges. If you want, you can also share if you practiced the Feeling-Breath-Thought-Skill strategy and how that went for you.

Activity

Equal Measurements

Sometimes, when we have a small rock challenge, we might have a huge volcano response. Let me give you an example. I was going to lunch, and they ran out of pizza. I was REALLY looking forward to pizza because I love it, so I screamed at the lunch lady, threw down my tray, and kicked the milk cart. What type of challenge is running out of pizza? And did my response match the challenge? What about if the opposite happens? What about when there's a huge volcano challenge and we only have a small rock response? For example, there is a fire, and I ignore it to keep playing on my tablet. What type of challenge is a fire? And does my response of playing on my tablet match the challenge size? Now, let's practice some **Equal Measurements** in your workbook. We will measure the challenges and see if the responses match or not. If it's a match, we will circle it. If it's not a match, we will cross it out.

What can you do if your challenge and response don't measure up equally? You can practice F-B-T-S! *Review **F-B-T-S poster** and continue to expand upon the concept by incorporating measuring challenges and problem-solving with it this week:*

- Name your **feeling**: "I am feeling _____," because my problem is " _____."

- Take three slow, deep **breaths**.

- Choose helpful, happy **thoughts**. "This is just a feeling. It will pass. I will be okay. This is a big hill challenge. I will get some help to handle this!"

- Pick a **skill** to practice. "I choose to do _____."

This week, when you are faced with a challenge, ask yourself what type of challenge it is and check to see if your response matches the challenge. If not, what skill will you choose to cool down?

Weekly Skills

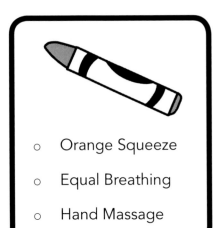

- ○ Orange Squeeze
- ○ Equal Breathing
- ○ Hand Massage

Our first skill this week is called **Orange Squeeze**. Imagine you are holding oranges in both of your hands and squeeze the oranges as tightly as you can to make orange juice. Hold the squeeze for ten seconds and squeeze every last drop out. Now, relax your hands. Can you feel the difference between feeling tense and feeling relaxed? Now, breathe in and squeeze the oranges, and then breathe out and let the oranges drop.

Our second skill is called **Equal Breathing.** Breathe in through your nose while counting to four in your head. Breathe out through your nose while counting to four in your head. You want to match the size of your inhale to the size of your exhale, as you take slow, deep breaths through your nose.

After Orange Squeeze, this is a great one! It's called **Hand Massage**. Hold your left hand in your right hand and put your right thumb on the pad of your left palm under your pointer finger. Use your thumb to massage in circles, working your way from the inside to the outside of your palm. Next squeeze and pinch each finger. Now, flip your hand over and rub the top of it. Repeat on the other hand.

Give the children time to color the skills. Remember to provide them with transition warnings and use the visual schedule before moving on.

Wrap Up

We are wrapping up for today. We are going to end with a **Body Scan Mindful Moment** (page 116) and then do our **Feelings Check**. *Refer to the visual schedule.* I want to remind you that this is your sixth session. That means we are halfway done! It's important to keep practicing your skills at home. This week, you will continue to practice measuring your challenges and seeing if the measurement is equal to your response. When you are faced with a challenge this week, ask yourself what type of challenge is it and whether your response matches. Continue being a thought detective and practicing F-B-T-S.

*End with your **closing practice** and hand out the weekly **Family Resource**, if it applies to your setting.*

Equal Measurements

This week, we learned about matching our responses to our challenges so that they are equal. Sometimes, your child may have a "huge volcano" response to a "small rock" challenge. We practiced making equal measurements by matching the response with the challenge size. You can extend this learning at home by making up scenarios and responses and discussing whether or not they are equal measurements.

If your measurements aren't equal, it would be a great time to practice F-B-T-S:

- Name your **feeling**: "I am feeling _____," because my problem is "_____."

- Take three slow, deep **breaths**.

- Choose helpful, happy **thoughts.** "This is just a feeling. It will pass. I will be okay. This is a big hill challenge. I can get some help to handle this!"

- Pick a **skill** to practice. "I choose _____."

Avoidance and Anxiety

It is an entirely natural response to want to avoid something that doesn't make you feel good. However, if you let your child avoid something that makes them feel upset, while it may temporarily decrease upset feelings, their feelings will become more intense and more problematic to deal with later. Your child may begin to experience anticipatory anxiety, and it will be even harder to cope with. Examples of this would include lingering at the doorway at the school drop-off zone because your child doesn't want you to leave, or letting your child stay home from school because they were teased yesterday. Another example is leaving a park because a dog is nearby as your child feels upset around dogs. Researchers have noted that avoiding situations that increase anxiety "stops children from mastering appropriate coping skills and maintains anxiety in the long term."[7]

The takeaway here is not to let your child avoid everything they are afraid of. If your child has a phobia, they will benefit from working with a professional to directly address it. Otherwise, have your child practice Feeling-Breath-Thought-Skill (F-B-T-S) and use the skills they are learning. Validate their feelings and encourage them by saying something affirming (e.g., "I know you can do this," "You are going to get really good at handling difficult things and calming yourself down," "I know you have the tools to deal with your big feelings!").

Consider making up a family motto with a positive self-talk phrase embedded into it, such as "in this family, we are problem-solvers!" When your children come to you with an issue, you can remind them of the motto, allowing them to empower themselves to solve their own problems. They may impress you with their solutions.

---

[7] Kendall, P. C., Swan, A. J., Carper, M. M., & Hoff, A. L. (2018). Anxiety disorders among children and adolescents. In J. N. Butcher & P. C. Kendall (Eds.), *APA handbooks in psychology®. APA handbook of psychopathology: Child and adolescent psychopathology* (pp. 213–230). American Psychological Association.

Skills to Practice This Week

Orange Squeeze

Imagine you are holding oranges in both of your hands and squeeze the oranges as tightly as you can to make orange juice. Hold the squeeze for ten seconds and squeeze every last drop out. Now, relax your hands. Can you feel the difference between feeling tense and feeling relaxed? Now, breathe in and squeeze the oranges, and then breathe out and let the oranges drop.

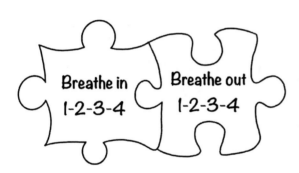

Equal Breathing

Breathe in through your nose while counting to four in your head. Breathe out through your nose while counting to four in your head. You want to match the size of your inhale to the size of your exhale as you take slow, deep breaths through your nose.

Hand Massage

Hold your left hand in your right and put your right thumb on the pad of your left palm under your pointer finger. Use your thumb to massage in circles, working your way from the inside to the outside of your palm. Next, squeeze and pinch each finger. Now, flip your hand over and rub the top of it. Repeat on the other hand.

My Relaxing Happy Place

Outline

o Opening practice, agreements & visual schedule

o Mindful Moment & Feelings Check: *Relaxing Happy Place* (p. 124)

o Activity: My Relaxing Happy Place

o Weekly Skills: Bumble Bee Breath, Door Squeeze & Unicorn Breath

o Mindful Moment & Feelings Check: *Muscle Relaxation* (p. 118)

o Closing Practice & Family Resource

Additional Materials

☐ Balloon (be aware of latex allergies)

☐ Measuring Challenges poster

Introduction

Start the session with your **opening practice,** *and then review your* **group agreements** *and your* **visual schedule.**

Mindful Moment & Feelings Check

Ask the children to do a self-scan. Use a visual if needed. Then, read the **Relaxing Happy Place Mindful Moment** *(page 124) followed by a* **Feelings Check,** *during which you can also do a brief review of the previous week:* Last week, we learned about matching our challenges with our responses so that they are equal. *Review the* **Measuring Challenges poster.** As we check-in with how we are feeling right now, if anyone wants to share what they noticed over the past week when they measured any of their challenges and responses, let us know; and how did it go with practicing Feeling-Breath-Thought-Skill this week?

Activity

My Relaxing Happy Place

We started with a relaxation to visualize your relaxing happy place. To visualize something means to imagine a picture of it in your mind. You can close your eyes and take some slow, deep breaths and visualize your relaxing happy place at any time or place! When you close your eyes to imagine something, try to use all of your senses. What do you see there? Are there other people around? What noises do you hear? What is the temperature? What does it feel like? Are there any smells or tastes?

Visualizing relaxing places or things that make you happy is a great skill to use when you're feeling overwhelmed because your body doesn't know the difference between visualizing and experiencing something! If you were thinking unhelpful thoughts, like "what if thoughts," your body might react and get tense, but if you visualize something positive or happy, your body will start to relax and feel calm.

When do you think it would be a good time to close your eyes and imagine your relaxing happy place? *Allow children to respond.* What about if you were on a very loud bus? If you were nervous before a test? If you had big feelings after getting yelled at?

Now, I want you to take some time and either draw or write about your own **relaxing happy place** in your workbook. Remember, there is no right or wrong way to do this. This is your special workbook, just for you!

If time allows, have the children talk about their relaxing happy place or share their drawings if they want to.

*Take out the **F-B-T-S poster and balloon**.* This week, before we move on to our skills, we are going to play F-B-T-S Balloon Bop! We are going to spread out around the room. Please be aware of the space around you, so you don't get too close to anyone. We will work together as a team to try to keep the balloon off the floor. Each time someone bops the balloon, we will chant together repeating one letter or word with each bop: "F-B-T-S, Feeling-Breath-Thought-Skill." If the balloon touches the floor, we won't get upset because that's a small rock challenge, and we know it's okay to make mistakes! *Review the **Measuring Challenges poster**.*

o   Bumble Bee
    Breath

o   Door Squeeze

o   Unicorn Breath

Weekly Skills

This week, our first skill is called **Bumble Bee Breath**. If you don't like loud noises, you might not like this one, but please give it a try if you are comfortable. With your lips sealed firmly, take a deep breath in through your nose. Now breathe out and make an "mmm" sound like a bumble bee buzzing. Try to buzz as long as you can. If you are comfortable, you can try it again while covering your ears.

Our next skill is called **Door Squeeze**. Pretend you are playing hide-and-seek with your friends, and you want to sneak through a small gap in a door quietly. Sit or stand up very tall and straight and suck your stomach in. Good! Now, hold your stomach tightly for 10 seconds to make it through the door. Remember to continue to breathe as you hold your stomach muscles tightly! Okay, now relax and unclench your stomach.

Our last skill this week is called **Unicorn Breath**. Place your pointer finger on the sparkle. Trace the unicorn horn down the right side as you breathe in through your nose. Next, trace the bottom of the unicorn horn from right to left as you hold your breath in. Finally, trace the unicorn horn up from the bottom to top as you breathe out. Repeat and feel the unicorn sparkle!

Give the children time to color the skills. Remember to provide them with transition warnings and use the visual schedule before moving on.

Wrap Up

We are wrapping up for today. We will end with a **Muscle Relaxation Mindful Moment** (page 118) and then do our **Feelings Check**. *Refer to the visual schedule.* This week, practice F.B.T.S., visualizing your relaxing happy place, and practice measuring your challenges.

*End with your **closing practice** and hand out the weekly **Family Resource**, if it applies to your setting.*

My Relaxing Happy Place

This week we practiced visualizing our relaxing happy places. Ask your child if they want to share about their relaxing happy place. Visualization is a powerful yet simple tool. You can remind your child that they can use this skill anywhere and at any time. When we do visualizations, we try to tap into all of our senses. What do you see, smell, or taste? Are there other people around? What noises do you hear? What is the temperature in your relaxing happy place? What does it feel like?

You can extend the learning at home this week by looking up and practicing some guided visualizations with your child. You can also write a guided visualization together. A helpful resource to listen to visualizations can be found in the references below.[8]

Flexibility

You can encourage your child's flexibility by giving positive feedback when you observe your child being a flexible thinker: "You wanted fries, but we only have broccoli left. I like how you used your skills and were such a flexible thinker here and ate your broccoli without an issue!" If your child struggles with changes to routines or transitions, you can remind them that you would like them to practice being a flexible thinker before a transition.

You can model being a flexible thinker and using F-B-T-S yourself. In situations where it is appropriate, it can be beneficial for children to hear you think your thought process aloud: e.g., "I wanted to see the movie at 10:30, but it's not playing at our usual theater. I feel annoyed, but I will stay positive and be a flexible thinker, and switch our schedule to see the movie at the other theater instead."

---

[8] CHOC Children's. (n.d.) *Guided Imagery*. CHOC Children's. https://www.choc.org/programs-services/integrative-health/guided-imagery/

You can challenge your child to play the flexible-thinking game. Ask them to think of and do as many things as differently as possible, such as brushing their teeth with the opposite hand, taking a different route to school, switching where they usually sit on the couch, or completing things in a different order than usual.

Additional ideas to encourage flexibility are as follows:

- Discuss a problem and brainstorm a list of as many different ways to solve it as possible.

- Play a game you usually play, but change one of the rules.

- Use a rock and some dough to show the difference between flexibility and inflexibility. Show how you can make creative and interesting shapes with the dough because of its flexibility.

- Play a game in which you try to think of as many different uses for a random object as possible. Be extra silly with this one!

- Play a game in which you create a story one line at a time. Have one person begin the story with a single line, and then pass the story to the next person, who adds on a line, and so on.

- Point out when characters are showing flexible or inflexible thinking in TV shows or movies.

- Read some of these books with your children on flexible thinking:

    o *Your Fantastic Elastic Brain* by JoAnn Deak

    o *Bubble Gum Brain* by Julia Cook

    o *My Day is Ruined! A Story Teaching Flexible Thinking* by Bryan Smith and Lisa Griffin

Skills to Practice This Week

Bumble Bee Breath

With your lips sealed firmly, take a deep breath in through your nose. Now, breathe out and make an "mmm" sound like a bumble bee buzzing. Try to buzz as long as you can. If you are comfortable, you can try it again while covering your ears.

Door Squeeze

Imagine you are playing hide-and-seek with your friends, and you want to sneak through a door quietly. Sit or stand up very tall and straight and suck your stomach in. Now, hold your stomach tightly for ten seconds to make it through the door. Remember to continue to breathe as you hold your stomach muscles tightly! Okay, now relax and unclench your stomach.

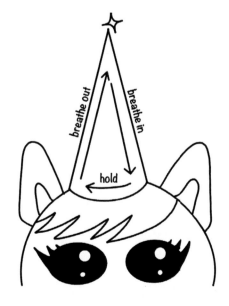

Unicorn Breath

Place your pointer finger on the sparkle. Trace the unicorn horn down the right side as you breathe in through your nose. Next, trace the bottom of the unicorn horn from right to left as you hold your breath in. Finally, trace the unicorn horn up from the bottom to top as you breathe out. Repeat and feel the unicorn sparkle!

My Sunny Breathing Words

Outline

- Opening practice, agreements & visual schedule

- Mindful Moment & Feelings Check: *My Sunny Breathing Words* (p. 125)

- Activity: My Sunny Breathing Words

- Weekly Skills: Ice Cream Twist, Finger Aerobics & Counting for Calm

- Mindful Moment & Feelings Check: *Gentle Body Movements* (p. 120)

- Closing Practice & Family Resource

Additional Materials

- ☐ Balloon (be aware of latex allergies)

Introduction

*Start with your **opening practice,** and then review your group **agreements** and your **visual schedule**.*

Mindful Moment & Feelings Check

*Ask the children to do a self-scan. Use a visual if needed. Then, read the **Sunny Breathing Words Mindful Moment** (page 125) followed by a **Feelings Check**, during which you can also do a brief review of the previous week:* Last week, we practiced visualizing our relaxing happy places. As we check-in with our feelings this week, you can share what you noticed when you practiced visualizing your relaxing happy place, or when you practiced Feeling-Breath-Thought-Skill over the week.

Activity

My Sunny Breathing Words

This week, we are learning about Sunny Breathing. During our Mindful Moment, I said some different words and phrases. Sunny Breathing is when we pair a short word or phrase with slow, deep breaths and repeat the words silently in our minds until we feel calm. It helps to use a word that has two parts, or syllables, or two short words that are one syllable each. *Children may benefit from clapping out syllables here.*

If we use two short words or a word with two parts, we can think about one part on the inhale, or the breath in, and the other part on the exhale, or the breath out. When we practice this Mindful Moment, we just think the sunny words in our head; we don't say them out loud. For example, breathe in and think "re," and breathe out and think "lax." Or breathe in and think "here," and breathe out and think "now."

Let's turn in our workbooks to the page with **My Sunny Breathing Words** on it. Circle all the words you would like to try Sunny Breathing with. Write the word or words you like the most inside the sun. You can add your own Sunny Breathing words to try, too!

When do you think it would be a good time to practice Sunny Breathing? Where could you practice Sunny Breathing? When you are using F-B-T-S, Sunny Breathing would be a great skill to use at the end! I like to practice Sunny Breathing and keep repeating my word with my breath, until my whole body feels calm. *Review the F-B-T-S poster. You might want to have a balloon prepared because the children will likely ask to play F-B-T-S Balloon Bop again!*

Weekly Skills

Our first skill this week is a little tricky. It's called **Ice Cream Twist**. If you don't get it at first, don't worry! It's okay to make mistakes, and this one takes a lot of practice. Stand up and cross one ankle over the other. Put your arms out straight in front of you, and then turn your thumbs towards the floor so your palms are facing out. Cross one wrist over the other and interlace your fingers together. Then, turn your hands in towards your heart. Breathe in and out through your nose

- o Ice Cream Twist
- o Finger Aerobics
- o Counting for Calm

slowly as you place your tongue on the top of your mouth. Untwist yourself and try again by crossing your ankles and wrists in the opposite direction.

Our next skill for today is called **Finger Aerobics**. This is another really fun skill to use. Start with an open hand. Breathe in and out through your nose while touching your thumb to your pinky. Breathe in and out through your nose while touching your thumb to your ring finger. Breathe in and out through your nose while touching your thumb to your middle finger. Breathe in and out through your nose while touching your thumb to your pointer finger. Switch hands and try it again. Then, try it with both hands at the same time.

Our last skill this week is called **Counting for Calm**. You are going to think about the numbers as you breathe. So, we are going to count ten slow, deep breaths. Then, count backward from ten to one. Breathe slowly and deeply while you think about each number. When you try this at home, if you want to experiment and try something new, you can try skip-counting while breathing.

Next, give the children time to color the skills. Remember to provide them with transition warnings and use the visual schedule before moving on.

Wrap Up

We are wrapping up for today, and we will end with a **Gentle Body Movements Mindful Moment** (page 120) and then do our **Feelings Check**. *Refer to the visual schedule.* Try to practice your Sunny Breathing Words this week, along with F-B-T-S.

*End with your **closing practice** and hand out the weekly **Family Resource**, if it applies to your setting.*

Sunny Breathing

This week, we learned about Sunny Breathing, which is when you pair a short word or phrase (such as "be calm") with slow, deep breaths. You repeat the words in your mind while synchronizing each part of the word or phrase with your breath. For example, you can inhale and think "be" and exhale and think "calm." You and your child can brainstorm a list of both silly and calming words to use this skill with.

Media Exposure and Attentional Bias

In week two we addressed how media can be a trigger for some children and we will briefly explore that here. Attentional bias means that people pay attention to some things and ignore other things. Sadly, we live in an era where we can't control everything our children are exposed to, such as scary events at school like lockdown drills or bomb threats. However, many children worry about things they overhear their family members talking about or issues they see on TV, such as violence on the news. Due to the attentional bias that many children have toward threats, it is important to have age-appropriate boundaries around what you share with your children. You also want to monitor how much and what type of media content your child has access to. A recent study on children's use of tablets in the home suggested that unmonitored use of tablets can have a negative impact on children, especially in terms of "reduced social interaction, fatigue, and increased family tensions due to excessive usage."[9]

---

[9] Hadlington, L., White, H. and Curtis, S. (2019). "I cannot live without my [tablet]": Children's experiences of using tablet technology within the home. *Computers in Human Behavior, 94,* 19-24. https://doi.org/10.1016/j.chb.2018.12.043

In terms of what media content children are exposed to, 89 percent of the top-selling video games contain violent content, and almost half of that was considered serious in nature. [10] The American Academy of Pediatrics (AAP) has stated that there are many negative outcomes associated with media violence, including "aggressive behavior, desensitization to violence, nightmares, and fear of being harmed." [11] The AAP recommends media time for children two to five years old to be less than one hour per day of "high-quality programming." For children older than six years old, they suggest that parents put "consistent limits" on media types and times, while ensuring that media use does not replace other activities like sleep and physical activity. They also encourage having certain times and places in the home that are media-free.

---

[10] Media Education Foundation. (n.d.) *Media violence: facts and statistics.* https://www.mediaed.org/handouts/ChildrenMedia.pdf

[11] American Academy of Pediatrics (2016, October 21). *American academy of pediatrics announces new recommendations for children's media use.* Healthy Children. https://www.healthychildren.org/English/news/Pages/AAP-Announces-New-Recommendations-for-Childrens-Media-Use.aspx

Skills to Practice This Week

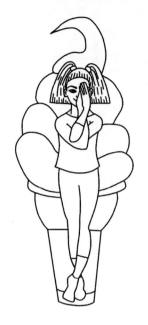

Ice Cream Twist

Stand up and cross one ankle over the other. Put your arms out straight in front of you, and then turn your thumbs towards the floor so your palms are facing out. Cross one wrist over the other and interlace your fingers together. Then, turn your hands in towards your heart. Breathe in and out through your nose slowly as you place your tongue on the top of your mouth. Untwist yourself and try crossing your ankles and wrists in the opposite direction.

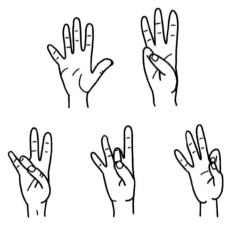

Finger Aerobics

Start with an open hand. Breathe in and out through your nose while touching your thumb to your pinky. Breathe in and out through your nose while touching your thumb to your ring finger. Breathe in and out through your nose while touching your thumb to your middle finger. Breathe in and out through your nose while touching your thumb to your pointer finger. Switch hands and try it again. Then, try it with both hands at the same time.

Counting for Calm

Count ten slow, deep breaths while you think about each number. Then, count backward from ten to one while breathing slowly and deeply. You can also try skip-counting while breathing if you want to experiment. Repeat until you feel calm.

Positive Self-Talk

Outline

o Opening practice, agreements & visual schedule

o Mindful Moment & Feelings Check: *Positive Self-Talk* (p. 126)

o Activity: Positive Self-Talk

o Weekly Skills: Sandy Toes, High-Five Breath & Strong Tree Blowing

o Mindful Moment & Feelings Check: *Breathe in Relaxation* (p. 114)

o Closing Practice & Family Resource

Additional Materials

No additional materials needed this week.

Introduction

*Start with your **opening practice**, and then review your group **agreements** and your **visual schedule**.*

Mindful Moment & Feelings Check

*Ask the children to do a self-scan. Use a visual if needed. Then read the **Positive Self-Talk Mindful Moment** (page 126) followed by a **Feelings Check**, during which you can also do a brief review of the previous week:* Last week, we learned about visualizing our relaxing happy places. As we check-in with our feelings this week, you can also share what you noticed when you practiced visualizing your relaxing happy place or when you practiced your Feeling-Breath-Thought-Skill strategy over the week.

Activity

Positive Self-Talk

We have been learning about helpful thoughts, and today we will learn about positive self-talk. Positive self-talk involves having some useful words or phrases you can repeat, or think to yourself, to help make you feel better when you are having big feelings or feeling stuck. This is really useful when you know one of your triggers will be happening soon. We can't avoid our triggers. We need to face them to get good at dealing with them. So, if one of my triggers is waiting in lines and I know there will be many lines during the holiday season when I need to do a lot of shopping, I will repeat to myself, "I know I can handle this! I have dealt with lines before, and I can do it again!"

Do you have any positive self-talk that you use now? What positive self-talk words or phrases would be most helpful for you? When do you think it would be a good time to practice positive self-talk? Where could you practice positive self-talk?

Turn to the **Positive Self-Talk** page in your workbook, and we will work through the exercise together. Circle the positive self-talk examples that you like the most; or those you think will be the most helpful for you. You can also write down your own positive self-talk in the blank bubbles.

Can you remember what F-B-T-S stands for without looking at the poster?

- Name your **feeling**: "I am feeling _____."

- Take 3 slow, deep **breaths**.

- Choose helpful, happy **thoughts** or positive self-talk. "I can do this!"

- Pick a **skill** to practice. "I choose _____."

Weekly Skills

- o Sandy Toes
- o High-Five Breath
- o Strong Tree Blowing

Our first skill this week is a stretch for your legs and feet. It's called **Sandy Toes**. Imagine you are barefoot at a beautiful beach, standing in the sand near the shoreline. Bend your knees to press your legs and feet as far down into the sand as you can. Curl and press your toes down into the sand and hold for ten seconds. Good! Now shake your feet and legs out and feel them loosen and relax.

Our next skill for today is called **High-Five Breath**. Open your hand up like you are going to give a high-five. Take your other pointer finger and place it at the base of your thumb. Slide up your thumb slowly as you breathe in and slide down your thumb slowly as you breathe out. Repeat this movement and breathing for each finger. Then, trace the other hand.

Our last skill for today is called **Strong Tree Blowing**. Imagine it is a very windy day, and you are a strong tree that is slowly blowing back and forth in the wind. Reach your arms up above your head as you breathe in. Interlace your fingers above your head. Bend at the waist to your left as you breathe out. Breathe in and come back to the center. Now, breathe out and bend at the waist to your right. Breathe in and come back to the center. Lower your arms down slowly by your side.

Give the children time to color the skills. Remember to provide them with transition warnings and use the visual schedule before moving on.

Wrap Up

We are wrapping up for today. We will end with a **Breathe in Relaxation Mindful Moment** (page 114) and then do our **Feelings Check**. *Refer to the visual schedule.* I want to remind you that today was our ninth session, so that means we have three sessions left. Please keep practicing F-B-T-S and your positive self-talk this week.

*End with your **closing practice** and hand out the weekly **Family Resource**, if it applies to your setting.*

Positive Self-Talk

This week, we learned about positive self-talk, which is having some useful words or phrases that you can repeat or think to yourself to soothe you. Positive self-talk makes you feel better when you are having big feelings, feeling stuck, or upset. Positive self-talk is also useful when your child knows one of their triggers will be happening soon. Since children can't avoid their triggers, this will be another skill they can use when facing their fears. Positive self-talk will help them feel more confident when dealing with challenges. To extend this week's learning at home, you can develop some positive self-talk phrases with your child.

Movement

In recent years, many children are becoming more sedentary. This is concerning because movement and physical activity benefit not only the body, but also the "brain structure, brain function, cognition, and [children's] school achievement." [12] The link between mental health and movement is being studied more each year. A recent study demonstrated that children with zero days per week of physical activity were about twice more likely to have anxiety.[13] In addition, European researchers conducted a study of over 11,000 adolescents and found that sports participation and frequent physical activity both "independently contribute to greater well-being and lower levels of anxiety and depressive symptoms." [14]

---

[12] Chaddock-Heyman, L., Hillman, C. H., Cohen, N. J. & Kramer, A. F. (2014). The importance of physical activity and aerobic fitness for cognitive control and memory in children. *Monographs of the Society for Research in Child Development, 79*(14), 25-50. https://doi.org/10.1111/mono.12129

[13] Zhu, X., Heagele, J. A. & Healy, S. (2019) Movement and mental health: behavioral correlates of anxiety and depression among children of 6-17 years old in the U.S. *Mental Health and Physical Activity 16*, 60-65. https://doi.org/10.1016/j.mhpa.2019.04.002

[14] McMahon, E. M., Corcoran, P., O'Regan, G., Keeley, H., Cannon, M., Carli, V., Wasserman, C., Hadlaczky, G., Sarchiapone, M., Apter, A., Balazs, J., Balint, M., Bobes, J., Brunner, R., Cozman, D., Haring, C., Iosue, M., Kaess, M., Kahn, J., ... Wasserman, D. (2017). Physical activity in European adolescents and associations

The takeaways here are that physical activity and movement are beneficial for improving both the body and the brain. Ensure that your child is getting enough movement and physical activity every day, whether that means running around the backyard, dancing, jumping on a trampoline, or playing sports.

with anxiety, depression and well-being. *European Child and Adolescent Psychiatry, (1)*111. https://www.doi.org/10.1007/s00787-016-0875-9

Skills to Practice This Week

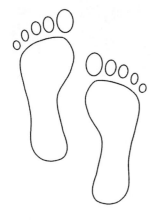

Sandy Toes

Imagine you are barefoot at a beautiful beach, standing in the sand near the shoreline. Bend your knees to press your legs and feet as far down into the sand as you can. Curl and press your toes down into the sand and hold for ten seconds. Then, shake your feet and legs out and feel them loosen and relax.

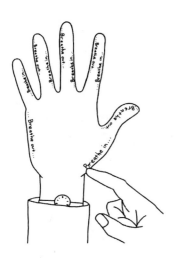

High-Five Breath

Open your hand up like you are going to give a high-five. Take your other pointer finger and place it at the base of your thumb. Slide up your thumb slowly as you breathe in and slide down your thumb slowly as you breathe out. Repeat this movement and breathing for each finger. Then, trace the other hand.

Strong Tree Blowing

It is a very windy day, and you are a strong tree that is slowly blowing back and forth in the wind. Reach your arms up above your head as you breathe in. Interlace your fingers above your head. Bend at the waist to your left as you breathe out. Breathe in and come back to the center. Now, breathe out and bend at the waist to your right. Breathe in and come back to the center. Lower your arms down slowly by your side.

Mistakes and Supports

Outline

- Opening practice, agreements & visual schedule

- Mindful Moment & Feelings Check: *Hot Air Balloon Ride* (p. 127)

- Activity: My Supports

- Weekly Skills: Tap Tap Squeeze, Flip Flop Nostril Breath & Letting Go

- Mindful Moment & Feelings Check: *Body Scan* (p. 116)

- Closing Practice & Family Resource

Additional Materials

- ☐ Measuring Challenges poster

Introduction

*Start with your **opening practice**, and then review your group **agreements** and your **visual schedule**.*

Mindful Moment & Feelings Check

*Ask the children to do a self-scan. Use a visual if needed. Then, read the **Hot Air Balloon Ride Mindful Moment** (page 127) followed by a **Feelings Check**, during which you can also do a brief review of the previous week:* Last week, we learned about positive self-talk. When we do our Feelings Check, you can also share if you used positive self-talk or if you practiced your Feeling-Breath-Thought-Skill strategy this week and how that went for you.

Activity

Mistakes and My Supports

When you first started to learn how to write your name, were you able to write all the letters the very first time perfectly without practicing? No! Why? Because you needed to practice over and over again. Part of practicing involves making mistakes. Mistakes are how we learn. I make mistakes all the time. Every single day, I make tons of mistakes! Is it okay to make mistakes? Yes! Mistakes are how we learn and grow! Pencils have erasers because they know that everyone is supposed to make mistakes. No one is perfect! If you try to get things to be perfect, you will feel frustrated a lot of the time.

What type of challenge is making a mistake on your math worksheet? *Review the* **Measuring Challenges poster** *if needed.* What about making a mistake on your spelling test? What about calling someone the wrong name? What about accidentally bumping into someone? When you make a mistake, how do you respond?

If I am learning a new way to do a math problem and I keep making mistakes, I can tell myself, "this is hard, but I won't give up, I will keep trying until I get it! It's okay to make mistakes. Mistakes are how we learn!" Let's review our F-B-T-S strategy today and see if we can do it again without looking at the poster. If we can't remember it, that's okay! We are still learning! *Review F-B-T-S, while incorporating making mistakes into the helpful thoughts this week.*

- Name your **feeling**: "I am feeling _____."

- Take three slow, deep **breaths**.

- Choose helpful, happy **thoughts**. "It's okay to make mistakes!"

- Pick a **skill** to practice. "I choose _____."

What do you do if you keep making the same mistake over and over again? You ask for help. Today, we are going to talk about your supportive person, or people, in your life. I want you to think for a minute about who supports you. Who is in your corner and always wants what is best for you?

Let's turn to the **My Supports** page in your workbook now. You can draw a picture or write the name of the person or people who support you. If you can, try to think of people in different parts of your life—in school, home, and outside activities. Maybe your family and friends support you at home and at school. Perhaps there are other people from outside activities who also support you, like those you see during sports, at church, or in other activities. When you think about the people who support you, how do you feel?

- o Tap Tap Squeeze
- o Flip Flop Nostril Breath
- o Letting Go

Weekly Skills

Our first skill this week is an awesome one! It's fun and also very calming to your body. It's called **Tap Tap Squeeze.** Watch me first, and then we'll do it together. Tap your right hand to your left shoulder and think of the word "I." Tap your left hand to your right shoulder and think of the word "am." Then, squeeze both hands together and think of the word "calm." Repeat the motion while thinking the phrase "I am calm" with each movement.

The next skill can be a little tricky. It takes a lot of practice, but it is a very calming skill once you figure it out. If you aren't able to get it today, don't worry! It will become easier with practice. It has a silly name—**Flip Flop Nostril Breath.** Watch me first, and then we'll practice together. Press your right thumb against your right nostril and breathe in slowly and deeply through your open left nostril. Then, lift your thumb up and place your pointer finger on the left nostril and breathe out and then breathe in through the right open nostril. Then, lift your pointer finger up and press your right thumb against your right nostril again, breathing out and in slowly and deeply through your open left nostril. Repeat in this pattern.

Our last skill for today is called **Letting Go.** It's a great skill to use if you are feeling upset or holding onto unhelpful thoughts. If you are comfortable, close your eyes, and visualize you are holding a balloon. Imagine blowing all of your big feelings into the balloon, tying the balloon, letting it go, and watching it float away into the sky. As the balloon floats away and disappears, you feel calmer and more peaceful.

Give the children time to color the skills. Remember to provide them with transition warnings and use the visual schedule before moving on.

Wrap Up

We are wrapping up our session for today. We will end with a **Body Scan Mindful Moment** (page 116) and then do our **Feelings Check**. *Refer to the visual schedule.* Remember, we only have two sessions left, and I want you to be practicing these skills even when you are feeling calm. This will make it easier to use the skills when you have big feelings. When you graduate from the group, you will bring your workbook home, and you will teach someone in your family the skills you learned. Don't worry; you don't need to teach them all at once! You can start thinking now about who you might like to teach the skills we've been learning. Maybe it will be someone who supports you at home, in school, or in other activities.

*End with your **closing practice**, and hand out the weekly **Family Resource**, if it applies to your setting.*

Mistakes and Supports

This week, we learned about the importance of making mistakes, since making mistakes are how we learn and grow. We also discussed our support systems. Identifying your support systems, or the supportive people in your life, is a great skill for children to learn. You can extend the learning at home by brainstorming different environments that your child spends time in and have them list supportive people in those other places.

Perfectionism and Making Mistakes

If a child strives for perfection, they will often feel frustrated or disappointed because perfection is impossible to achieve. When a child has perfectionistic tendencies, they may often get upset and either shut down or overreact when they make mistakes. You can help your child learn to be comfortable with making mistakes by talking about your own mistakes. You can also use the Measuring Challenges tool to help put small mistakes into perspective. For example, explain that you made a mistake by burning your eggs, which is a small rock problem, and you plan to resolve the issue by cooking more eggs.

You can also reinforce the concept that mistakes are okay by making statements, such as "mistakes are how we learn" and "It's okay to make mistakes." You can also talk to your children in an age-appropriate manner about some of your own mistakes and do some research together on some of the famous failures in society.

Be sure that you set realistic and age-appropriate expectations for your child. If you have unrealistic expectations for your child, this could lead to a fear of making mistakes, a fear of failure, or even procrastination. Sometimes, children who have perfectionistic tendencies may procrastinate to avoid making mistakes on a task or project. You can help your child by setting realistic goals and breaking them down into smaller, more manageable, steps so they don't feel overwhelmed.

Lastly, rather than praising your child by calling them smart, try to reinforce the *effort* they are displaying instead. For example, instead of calling them smart, you can comment on their work ethic. When you praise effort instead of ability, it helps children develop a growth mindset. A growth mindset will help your child stay more persistent with future obstacles. This change in how we praise our children is especially helpful for children who are perfectionists. For more information about growth mindset, please check out Carol Dweck and her colleagues' work at http://www.mindsetworks.com.

Skills to Practice This Week

Tap Tap Squeeze

Tap your right hand to your left shoulder and think of the word "I." Tap your left hand to your right shoulder and think of the word "am." Then, squeeze both hands together and think of the word "calm." Repeat the motion while thinking the phrase "I am calm" with each movement.

Flip Flop Nostril Breath

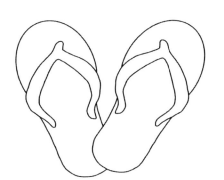

Press your right thumb against your right nostril and breathe in slowly and deeply through your open left nostril. Then, lift your thumb up and place your pointer finger on the left nostril and breathe out and then breathe in through the right open nostril. Then, lift your pointer finger up and press your right thumb against your right nostril again, breathing out and in slowly and deeply through your open left nostril. Repeat in this pattern.

Letting Go

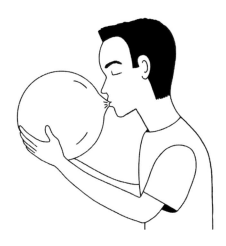

If you are comfortable, close your eyes and visualize you are holding a balloon. Imagine blowing all your big feelings into the balloon, tying the balloon, letting it go, and watching it float away into the sky. As the balloon floats away and disappears, you feel calmer and more peaceful.

Mindfulness and Gratitude

Outline

- o Opening practice, agreements & visual schedule

- o Mindful Moment & Feelings Check: *Present Moment* (p. 128)

- o Activity: Mindfulness & Gratitude

- o Weekly Skills: Shake Wiggle Shake, Starfish Breath & Steel to Jelly

- o Mindful Moment & Feelings Check: *Muscle Relaxation* (p. 118)

- o Closing Practice & Family Resource

Additional Materials

- ☐ Music with an excellent rhythm to shake to (such as drumming music)

Introduction

Start with your **opening practice,** and then review your group **agreements** and your **visual schedule.**

Mindful Moment & Feelings Check

Ask the children to do a self-scan. Use a visual if needed. Then, read the **Present Moment Mindful Moment** (page 128) followed by a **Feelings Check.** You can also do a brief review of the previous week: As we do our Feelings Check, feel free to share if you noticed anything over the week about making mistakes or your supports. Remember, next week is our last session, and then you will graduate! I am so excited for you! *Give the children the space to talk about their feelings about the group ending if they want to.*

Mindfulness and Gratitude

Activity

We practice Mindful Moments each week in this group, and, today, we are going to talk a little more about **mindfulness**. Does anyone have an idea of what that means? Mindfulness means paying attention, on purpose, to what is happening in the present moment—right here, right now—without judging it as being good or bad. It means just observing or noticing, and paying attention to what is happening, both inside and outside of you. That's why, when we do a Feelings Check, I ask you to think about how you are doing right now in this very moment. When we check-in on how we are right now, that is being mindful.

A lot of the skills we practice in these sessions help us become more mindful. If you are mindful, that means you aren't worried about what might happen in the future and aren't thinking about what happened in the past. You can be mindful while you are doing anything! You can be mindful doing schoolwork, coloring, eating, talking to someone, or even washing your hands. If you were being mindful when you washed your hands, you would be really focused on what you were doing, so you might be thinking about the temperature of the water, the smell of the soap, or how your hands feel rubbing together. When you are mindful, you are fully experiencing what you are doing in that moment. If you practice being mindful and paying attention to what is happening in the present moment, it will save you from many life challenges. No one can be mindful all the time; it's something we practice doing, and we get better at it the more we practice. Where could you practice being more mindful?

Does anyone know what being **grateful** means? Being grateful, or having gratitude, means that you realize what you are thankful for. Being mindful helps you to be more grateful. Thinking about what you are grateful for is a helpful, happy thought, so you feel good inside! Please turn to the **Mindfulness and Gratitude** page in your workbook. Let's talk about some of the things we are grateful for.

If time is limited, you can talk about the prompts on the page and have the children write them down later or at home. If time allows, you can pass a ball or bean bag around and when someone catches it, they can name something they are grateful for in the category you call out (e.g., place you are grateful for, food you are grateful for, person you are grateful for, book you are grateful for, toy you are grateful for, etc.)

Weekly Skills

- o Shake Wiggle Shake

- o Starfish Breath

- o Steel to Jelly

You will need to put on some music with a good rhythm for the first skill this week. Music by Babatunde Olatunji is always a good choice. Our first skill today is a super fun one! It's called **Shake Wiggle Shake**. Begin by shaking and wiggling one foot. Then, shake and wiggle the other foot. Then, shake and wiggle each leg. Then, shake and wiggle your hips. Then, shake and wiggle your hands, arms, and shoulders. Then, shake and wiggle your neck and head. Now your whole body is shaking and wiggling!

Now we will begin to calm ourselves down with **Starfish Breath**. You will need to take out your workbook for this one. Place your pointer finger on the baby starfish. Trace up as you breathe in and trace down as you breathe out. Trace the starfish pattern, breathing in and breathing out, as each arm of the starfish is traced, and you feel relaxed and calm.

Our last skill of the week is called **Steel to Jelly**. We have practiced a lot of tensing and then relaxing our muscles. It's helpful to be able to feel the difference between your body feeling tight and feeling relaxed. If you notice you are holding your muscles tightly, it's a sign you should practice your skills. Breathe in and tense all the muscles in your whole body as if they are made of steel. Tense your feet, legs, stomach, arms, hands, shoulders, neck, face, and jaw. As you slowly breathe out, relax and loosen all of your body's muscles as if they are turning from steel to jelly. Relax your feet, legs, stomach, arms, hands, shoulders, neck, and face.

Give the children time to color the skills. Remember to provide them with transition warnings and use the visual schedule before moving on.

Wrap Up

We are wrapping up for today. We will end with a **Muscle Relaxation Mindful Moment** (page 118) and then do our **Feelings Check**. *Refer to the visual schedule.* Remember, we only have one session left, and I want you to keep practicing your skills even when this group is over. When you graduate next week, you will bring home your workbook, and you will be teaching someone in your family all of the awesome skills you learned. When we do the Feelings Check today, please share who you are planning to teach your skills to when you bring your workbook home next week.

*End with your **closing practice,** and hand out the weekly **Family Resource,** if it applies to your setting.*

Mindfulness and Gratitude

This week, we learned about the importance of being grateful. We also learned about mindfulness. Being mindful means paying attention, on purpose, to what is happening in the present moment. When you are mindful, you aren't judging what is happening; you are just observing it. If you are mindful, it is hard to get swept away by unhelpful thoughts.

Having gratitude means that you realize what you are thankful for. Being mindful helps you be more grateful. You can continue this learning at home by creating moments to recognize gratitude. For example, you can choose a specific time of day (e.g., during dinner, after brushing teeth, etc.) when everyone shares one thing that they are grateful for.

Skills to Practice This Week

Shake Wiggle Shake

Put on some music and begin by shaking and wiggling one foot. Then, shake and wiggle the other foot. Then, shake and wiggle each leg. Then, shake and wiggle your hips. Then, shake and wiggle your hands, arms, and shoulders. Then, shake and wiggle your neck and head. Now your whole body is shaking and wiggling!

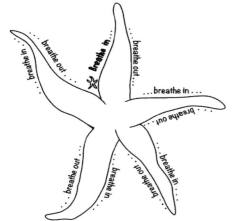

Starfish Breath

Place your pointer finger on the baby starfish. Trace up as you breathe in and trace down as you breathe out. Trace the pattern, breathing in and breathing out, as each arm of the starfish is traced, and you feel relaxed and calm.

Steel to Jelly

Breathe in and tense all the muscles in your whole body as if they are made of steel. Tense your feet, legs, stomach, arms, hands, shoulders, neck, face, and jaw. As you slowly breathe out, relax and loosen all of your body's muscles as if they are turning from steel to jelly. Relax your feet, legs, stomach, arms, hands, shoulders, neck, and face.

Closure

Outline

- Opening practice, agreements & visual schedule

- Mindful Moment & Feelings Check: *Bridge* (p. 128)

- Activity: In the Driver's Seat & My Favorite Skills

- Weekly Skills: Finger Lock, Cell Phone Breath & Grounding

- Mindful Moment & Feelings Check: *Gentle Body Movements* (p. 120)

- Closing Practice & Family Resource

Additional Materials

☐ Parent and Child Post-Group Survey (pages 137-138)

☐ Parent letter (page 33)

Introduction

*Start with your **opening practice,** and then review your group **agreements** and your **visual schedule**. Let the children know you may do things a little bit differently today since it's the last session.*

Mindful Moment & Feelings Check

*Ask the children to do a self-scan. Use a visual if needed. Then, read the **Bridge Mindful Moment** (page 128) followed by a **Feelings Check**, during which you can also do a brief review of the previous week:* Last week, we talked about being grateful and paying attention to the present moment by being mindful. Did anyone notice anything about mindfulness or gratitude this week? Did you use F-B-T-S this week and want to share how that was for you? How are you feeling about this being our last session?

Activity

In the Driver's Seat and My Favorite Skills

Today is a special day because it's our last session! Over the past twelve weeks, we have practiced so many new skills and learned how to cope with our big feelings! I am so excited and proud that today you are graduating from this group. I want you to keep practicing F.B.T.S. and the skills we've learned together. We are going to spend a few minutes doing a **Post-Group Survey** (page 137.) There are no right or wrong answers. Please be honest, because it will help me see what you've learned and help me run better sessions in the future.

Sometimes, when you feel overwhelmed or have big feelings, it might not seem like you have many choices, or it might not feel like you have a lot of things you can control. In times like this, it is useful to think about at least one thing that you can control. Let's look at the **In the Driver's Seat** activity in your workbook, and we will do this together. We will read each one, and then you will circle it if it's something you have control over or cross it out if it is something you don't have control over.

Complete activity with the group. Is there anything you noticed or that interested you about this activity?

Now, let's practice F-B-T-S before we practice our weekly skills. Who can say what F-B-T-S stands for without looking at the poster? *Review F-B-T-S while discussing closure.*

- Name your **feelings**: "I am feeling a little sad but also excited and proud that group is over."

- Take 3 slow, deep **breaths**.

- Choose helpful, happy **thoughts**. "It's hard that group is ending, but I learned so much and am so proud of how hard I worked!"

- Pick a **skill** to practice. "I choose Steel to Jelly."

Since it's our last session, we are going to do things a little bit differently. I need you all to practice being flexible thinkers! We will practice our three skills next, and then you will get to pick your top five favorite skills!

Weekly Skills

Our first skill today is called **Finger Lock.** Lift up your right arm straight up at heart level, and then bend it towards you. Point your right thumb down and curl your fingers in. Take your left arm and curl your left fingers underneath your right fingers. Breathe in as you pull your fingers against each other. Breathe out as you relax, soften, and release.

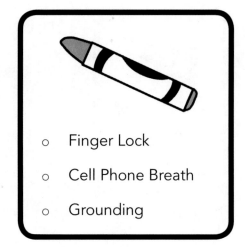

- o Finger Lock
- o Cell Phone Breath
- o Grounding

No matter where you go, there will probably always be someone with a cell phone nearby. This next skill is called **Cell Phone Breath.** You can practice with a real phone if you want, but you don't need an actual phone. You can also practice tracing on paper or even by tracing a rectangle shape on your palm. The tricky part of this breathing skill is holding your breath after you breathe out. So, it will take some practice to get good at this one. Please get out your workbooks so we can practice together. Start by placing your pointer finger on the star. Breathe in as you trace the cell phone up along the left side. Hold your breath in as you trace the top of the phone. Breathe out as you trace the right side of the phone. Now, hold your breath out as you trace along the bottom of the phone. Repeat.

Our last skill is called **Grounding.** It is a great skill to use if you are starting to feel overwhelmed or anxious, and it helps you practice being mindful. Look around you. Take a slow, deep breath. Use your senses to name five things you can see. Name four things you can touch. Name three things you can hear. Name two things you can smell, and name one thing you can taste.

Now, I want you to turn to the page that says **My Top Five Favorite Skills** in your workbook. Wow! Look at all the skills you've learned in our time together! Let's look at these pictures and see if we can work together to remember all of them. Now, I want you to pick your top five favorite skills and circle them. This will help you in the future, because when you use F-B-T-S, you'll probably want to choose one of your top five favorites for the skill part of it.

Wrap Up

We are wrapping up our last session! We will end with a **Gentle Body Movements Mindful Moment** (page 120) and then do our **Feelings Check**. *Refer to the visual schedule.*

This week, if you start to feel out of control or overwhelmed, you can try to focus on just one thing you can control. I like to focus on controlling my breath. I will be speaking with your families to tell them how awesome you did in our sessions and how proud I am of you! Remember, you get to bring your special workbooks home today, too! When we do our Feelings Check, please share who you will be teaching your skills to. If you'd like to share anything else about the sessions, or how you feel about them ending, you can share that as well.

*End with your **closing practice** and hand out the weekly **Family Resource,** including the **parent/guardian** letter (page 33) and **parent/guardian post-group surveys** (page 138), if it applies to your setting.*

Closure

Today was our last session together, and we talked about the importance of identifying what we have control over. This can help us when we have big feelings, are overwhelmed, or are feeling out of control. We also picked our top five favorite skills we have learned over the past twelve weeks in the group. Ask your child which skills they picked!

When children have big feelings, they might not feel like they have a lot of choices, or they might not feel like they have a lot of things they can control. In times like this, it is useful to brainstorm with them at least one thing that they can control in that moment. Giving a child very structured and limited choices such as sitting in the blue or red chairs may also be helpful. When children have too many options, it may cause them to feel overwhelmed.

Since transitions, or progressing from one activity to another, can be challenging for many children, you can give your child some control by using a timer. Time is a concept that can be hard for children to understand, so you can purchase a visual timer or find a visual timer app or website. Some children may need additional support with this. In this case, it may be helpful to problem-solve aloud with them what they can get done in that period of time. For example, they may benefit from a more concrete transition warning, such as adding ten more blocks to a tower before pausing to brush teeth, or finish reading the end of this paragraph before pausing to get a snack. You can also use a timer to make a non-preferred activity more fun, such as racing to see how many toys they can pick up in three minutes.

Caregiver Self-Care

All children act out or misbehave at some point, and when they do, it can be extremely stressful for parents and caregivers. Caregiver self-care is so important. The skills in this book were written in a fun, child-friendly way, but they will also work for adults! Please practice the skills with your children and find some healthy coping skills that work for you as well. There are some great relaxation apps available for adults and children. You can find a list at www.whole-childcounseling.com. It will go a long way as a caregiver when you model good self-care and know how to deal with your feelings appropriately. Please remember to have empathy, compassion, and forgiveness for yourself as well. At times, parenting can be trying.

Mindset Shift

Dr. Ross Greene from Lives in the Balance[15] writes about a simple but profound concept, which is, that kids would do well if they could do well: "In other words, if the kid had the skills to exhibit adaptive behavior, he wouldn't be exhibiting challenging behavior. That's because doing well is always preferable to not doing well." Dr. Greene has different parent training programs about his model. His belief that a child is not purposefully or deliberately acting out and that children, like the rest of us, do the best that they can do at any given moment, is an important concept.

Ideally, this mindset shift will help you not take things personally if your child acts out because you won't see their misbehavior as coming from a deliberate place. You can start being curious about their behavior instead and try to figure out what skills they need more help developing. Over the past twelve weeks, your child has learned *many* skills to handle big feelings, and, hopefully, with your guidance, they will continue practicing these skills and incorporating F-B-T-S at home.

---

[15] Greene, R. W. (2009). *Kids do well if they can*. Lives in the Balance. https://www.livesinthebalance.org/kids-do-well-if-they-can

Skills to Practice This Week

Finger Lock

Lift your right arm straight up at heart level, and then bend it towards you. Point your right thumb down and curl your fingers in. Take your left arm and curl your left fingers underneath your right fingers. Breathe in as you pull your fingers against each other. Breathe out as you relax, soften, and release.

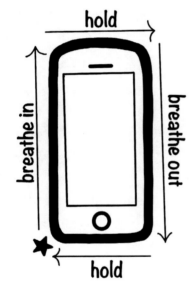

Cell Phone Breath

You can practice with a real phone if you want, but you don't need an actual phone. Start by placing your pointer finger on the star. Breathe in as you trace the cell phone up along the left side. Hold your breath in as you trace the top of the phone. Breathe out as you trace the right side of the phone. Now, hold your breath out as you trace along the bottom of the phone. Repeat.

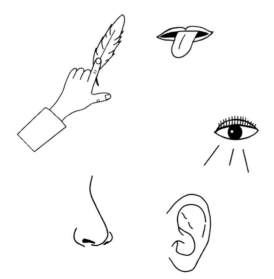

Grounding

Look around you. Take a slow, deep breath. Use your senses to name five things you can see. Name four things you can touch. Name three things you can hear. Name two things you can smell, and name one thing you can taste.

MINDFUL MOMENTS

Slow, Deep Belly Breaths (Session 1)

We will start our Mindful Moment with a self-scan. *Show the visual and remind the group what a self-scan means.* Notice what your body is doing. Please sit up straight with a quiet body and mouth. Place your hands on your knees or on your desk. Remember to do what works best for your own body here. As you sit up, you still want to feel comfortable and not too stiff. When we take a Mindful Moment, everything we do is a choice. I'm hoping you will try it, because the goal is to help you feel more relaxed, but you can sit quietly and wait for us to finish if you aren't ready just yet.

I invite you to place your hand on your belly and take the biggest breath of air you've taken in all day. Breathe in slowly and deeply, and feel your belly fill up with air. Now, breathe out slowly and deeply, and feel your belly fall. Breathe in and feel your belly rise. Breathe out and feel your belly fall.

Now, if you are comfortable, please close your eyes, and we'll try that with our eyes shut a couple of times. If you're not ready to close your eyes, you can gently soften your eyes or look down at your nose. Keep your hand on your belly, and feel it rise as you breathe in and fall as you breathe out. Practice on your own for a couple of breaths. *Pause.* Now, I welcome you to bring your attention back to this room and think about how you feel right now in this very moment. Please don't say the words out loud; just think them in your head. Stretch your arms in any way that feels good for you and gently open your eyes.

Debrief:
How did your first Mindful Moment feel? There are no right or wrong feelings. It might have been different for everyone. Just like exercise makes your muscles stronger, the brain acts like a muscle, so when we practice our Mindful Moments, we will get stronger and better at it. We will keep practicing together.

Breathe in Relaxation (Sessions 1, 5, and 9)

We will start our Mindful Moment with a self-scan. I want to invite you to sit up straight with a quiet body and mouth. Remember to please do what works best for your own body. As you sit up, you want to make sure you still feel comfortable and not too stiff. Everything is a choice, so you can sit quietly and wait for us to finish if you aren't ready just yet.

I welcome you to breathe in through your nose and relax your shoulders as you breathe out. Take a few more slow, deep breaths on your own. *Pause.* Now, if you are comfortable, you can close your eyes. If you're not ready yet, you can gently soften your eyes or look down at your nose.

Listen to my voice as you breathe in slowly…And breathe out slowly. Breathe in relaxation… Breathe out stress. Breathe in relaxation…Breathe out stress. Breathe in relaxation…Breathe out stress.

Now, try focusing on breathing in relaxation and breathing out stress on your own. If any other thoughts come into your mind, just let them go. Don't judge them; just let the thoughts float away like clouds in the sky. *Pause.*

Now, I want you to slowly bring your awareness back into this room and to my voice. Think of your body sitting in the chair and your feet supporting you. Think about how you feel right now, in this very moment. Don't say the feeling out loud. Just think it in your head. Okay, now gently flutter open your eyes.

Debrief:
How was that experience for you? How do you feel? Remember, there are no right or wrong feelings. It might have been different for everyone. Did anyone else have other thoughts that came up? That's totally normal! Our minds are very active. When I first started practicing Mindful Moments, I would get distracted with many other thoughts. I would be thinking about what I was going to eat for lunch that day or wondering what I might do that weekend. We will keep practicing, and it will get easier for us.

Wave Breath (Session 2)

I want to invite you to do a self-scan. Sit up straight with a quiet body and mouth, but please make sure you are comfortable and not too stiff. Breathe in and, as you breathe out, notice and relax your jaw, shoulders, and whole body. Our Mindful Moment today is a visualization called Wave Breath. To visualize something means to create a picture of it in your mind. I will ask you some questions, and you will think about the answers in your head.

Take a couple of cycles of slow, deep breaths. *Pause.* If you are comfortable, you can close your eyes. If you're not comfortable, you can gently soften your vision and look down at your nose. Listen to my voice as you breathe in slowly… And breathe out slowly. Allow yourself to become as relaxed as you can. Now, imagine you are at the beach on a beautiful summer day. You see the gorgeous ocean and the beautiful white sand. What else do you see there? *Pause.* Maybe there are people with you, or maybe you are alone. You can choose because this is your special beach trip. You can hear the sound of the ocean waves rolling against the shore and the wind lightly blowing. Far away, you can even hear the sounds of seagulls cawing in the distance as they fly around in the beautiful blue sky. Do you hear any other sounds? Maybe children are playing and laughing nearby, or some different sounds that make your heart feel good.

You can smell the saltwater from the ocean. You can feel the sand beneath your feet supporting you and the sun's rays warming your skin gently. If you choose to, you can walk towards the ocean and feel the cool, refreshing water splash against your toes and feet. Are there any tastes in your mouth? Is there a special treat you like to enjoy at the beach?

Now, breathe in as the beach waves splash on the shore and breathe out as the waves flow back into the water. Breathe in and watch the waves come in and splash on the sand; breathe out and watch the waves roll back towards the ocean. Try this on your own for a few more cycles of breath. Breathing with the waves. In and out. In and out. *Pause.*

Now, I want you to slowly bring your awareness back into this room and to my voice. Take a deep breath in and out. Think about how you feel right now. Slowly open your eyes and come back to the present.

Debrief:
How was that for you? Were you able to visualize the beach? How did it feel? Were you able to sync your breath with the waves?

Body Scan (Sessions 2, 6, and 10)

I want to invite you to start by doing a self-scan. Sit up straight with a quiet body and mouth. Please make sure you are comfortable and not too stiff. We are going to practice a body scan. That means we will be thinking about or paying attention to and noticing different parts of our body. We'll start with our feet and work our way up. Take a couple of slow, deep breaths in and out. *Pause.* If you are comfortable, I invite you to close your eyes. If you're not comfortable, you can gently soften your eyes or look down at your nose. We close our eyes because it helps us filter out all the distractions around us, so it can be a little easier to relax that way. Do what feels comfortable for you in this moment.

Try to clear your mind of any thoughts that enter and focus on my voice. If any thoughts pop into your head, just let them go and bring your attention back to your breath or my voice. Now, focus on and pay attention to your toes, your feet, and your ankles. Breathe in and out and notice how they feel. Next, focus on and pay attention to your legs and knees. Breathe in and out and notice how they feel. Focus on and pay attention to your lower back and belly. Breathe in and out deeply and notice how your belly rises and falls with your slow, deep breaths. Focus and pay attention to your arms, hands, and fingers. Breathe in and out and notice how they feel. Focus and pay attention to your shoulders and your upper back. Breathe in and out and notice how they feel. If there is any tension in your shoulders, try to let it go, and relax as you breathe in and out.

Lastly, I invite you to focus and pay attention to your neck, head, and face. Breathe in and out and notice how they feel. I invite you to try to loosen your jaw if there is any tightness there. Sit here for a moment with your whole body relaxed and calm, as you breathe in and out. *Pause.* Now, notice your body in the chair and check-in with yourself to see how you feel right now? Slowly open your eyes.

Debrief:
How was that for you? How did it feel? There are no right or wrong feelings. It might have been different for everyone, and that's okay! Did anyone else have other thoughts come up? That's fine! Thank you for being honest. If you do, I just want you to notice those thoughts without judging them.

Happy, Helpful Message (Session 3)

I want to invite you to do a self-scan. Sit up straight with a quiet body and mouth, but please make sure you are comfortable and not too stiff. I welcome you to breathe in through your nose and out through your mouth. We are going to do a visualization. Remember, this means you create a picture of something in your mind. Our visualization today is called Happy, Helpful Message. When we do a visualization, I'll ask some questions, but I want you to think of the answers in your head. You don't have to say the answers out loud.

Now, take a few cycles of slow, deep breaths. If you are comfortable, you can close your eyes. If you're not comfortable, you can gently soften your eyes and look down at your nose. Imagine that it is a gorgeous fall day, and you are taking a walk in the woods. You are surrounded by nature. The leaves on the trees look so beautiful around you. You can hear some birds chirping and some leaves crunching under your feet. What else do you see? *Pause.* You look up ahead and notice a river. You decide to take a walk along the river. You walk along the riverbank and match your breathing to your steps. You breathe in and take a step, breathe out and take a step. You pause, because you see a bottle with a cork in it that has been washed onto the shore. You pick it up and notice there is a paper rolled up inside. You have a feeling in your heart that there is a happy, helpful message inside the bottle, waiting for you. You pop the cork out and pull the paper out. You take a deep breath in and out as you unroll the paper. You read what the happy, helpful message says. *Pause.* Wow, this special message was just for you. You fold the paper up and put it in your pocket. You take a big, deep inhale to breathe your happy, helpful message in, and a big breath out to let all the stress from your body melt away. Again, you breathe in your happy, helpful message, and you breathe out any stress.

Now, I invite you to bring your attention back to your body in this room and to my voice. Shake your shoulders and wiggle your feet a little bit. Take a big breath in and think about how you are feeling. Breathe out and slowly open your eyes.

Debrief:
How was that for you? Does anyone want to share what their happy, helpful message was? If not, that's okay!

Muscle Relaxation (Sessions 3, 7, and 11)

I want to invite you to do a self-scan. Sit up straight with a quiet body and mouth, but please make sure you are comfortable and not too stiff. Remember to breathe slowly and deeply. Today, we are going to practice relaxing our muscles. This is like a body scan, but we will be tightening and then relaxing our muscles this time. Once again, we'll start with our feet and work our way up. Take a couple of slow, deep breaths in and out.

If you are comfortable, I invite you to close your eyes. If you're not comfortable, you can gently look down at your nose and soften your eyes. We close our eyes because it helps us filter out everything around us, so it can be easier for us to relax that way; but please do what feels comfortable for you right now, in this moment.

I invite you to try to let any thoughts float out of your mind. If they come back in again, just observe them. Try not to get sucked into your thoughts or get upset by them. Just try to bring your attention back to my voice.

Now, I invite you to think about your toes, your feet, and your ankles. Breathe in and tighten your feet. You might even point your feet forward and curl your toes in. You might feel the muscles in your leg working with you, too. Now, as you breathe out, let your toes and feet soften and relax. As we move on, I welcome you to notice the difference in your body between the tense and the relaxed sensations.

Next, let's focus on your legs and knees. I invite you to take a breath in and tighten all your leg muscles. Good. Now, as you breathe out, relax all those leg muscles. Feel your legs and knees soften and release.

Now, let's pay attention to your lower back and belly. Take a slow, deep breath in and out and notice how your belly rises and falls with your breath. On your next breath in, I invite you to tense your belly and lower back. Remember to always do what feels comfortable in your body. Now, as you breathe out, relax those lower back and belly muscles. Feel them soften and release.

Now, let's think about your arms, hands, and fingers. I welcome you to breathe in and tense your arms, hands, and fingers. You might even curl your hands into fists. On your next breath out, relax your arms, hands, and fingers. Feel them slowly soften and release.

Next, we'll focus on your shoulders and your upper back. Just a gentle reminder to only tighten however much feels right in your body. You don't want to overdo it. As you breathe in, tighten your shoulders and upper back. You might even lift your shoulders up toward your ears as you stiffen them. Now, as you breathe out, let all the tension in your shoulders and upper back relax. Feel them soften and release.

Lastly, I welcome you to notice your neck, head, jaw, and face. If it feels comfortable to you, tighten your neck, head, and face muscles on your next breath in. You might scrunch up your nose and even clench your teeth. Now, as you breathe out, relax all of those neck, head, jaw, and face muscles. Feel them soften and release.

Notice how your whole body feels now. There are no right or wrong sensations. Just observe. Now, I invite you to slowly bring your attention back to my voice. Bring your awareness to the fact that you are sitting in this room. Stretch your arms out slowly and gently open your eyes.

Debrief:
How was that for you? Were you able to feel the difference between the tense states and the relaxed sensations in your body? If not, that's okay. Remember, we will get better with practice. Being aware of what your body feels like when it is tight and tense is a useful skill, because if you notice when your body feels tight, you can use some of your skills to relax it.

Elephant Ears (Session 4)

I want to invite you to do a self-scan. Sit up straight with a quiet body and mouth, but please make sure you are comfortable and not too stiff. Breathe in and breathe out slowly and deeply.

In our Mindful Moment today, we will practice listening to all the different sounds we can hear. Take a few cycles of slow, deep breaths. If you are comfortable, you can close your eyes. If you're not comfortable, you can gently look down at your nose and soften your vision.

Breathe in and out slowly. Try to relax your whole body and get as comfortable as you can. Now, I invite you to picture in your mind what an elephant looks like. Elephants have huge ears which help them hear many different sounds, even from far away. Now, imagine that your hearing is as good as an elephant's hearing.

I welcome you to sit quietly and just listen. Notice any sounds you may hear. Think about the name of the sound, but try not to overthink it. Just listen to the sound, name it, and let it go. You may only hear silence, and that's okay, too. Maybe, if you hear silence all around, you will tune into the sound of your own quiet breathing. I'm going to give you some time to practice listening now. *Pause.*

Please bring your awareness back to this room. Listen to the sounds of your breath and the sound of my voice. Take a slow, deep breath in and out and think about how you feel in this moment. Slowly open your eyes, as you stretch your body in any way that feels comfortable for you and come back to the present.

Debrief:
How was that for you? What sounds did you notice? Were you able to stay focused on the sounds? Did you get distracted by your thoughts? If so, that's okay! Remember not to judge yourself. Most people do start thinking about other things. If you were able to hear silence, how did that feel to you?

Gentle Body Movements (Sessions 4, 8, and 12)

For this Mindful Moment, you will be sitting in a chair, or, if you are on the floor, please put your legs out straight in front of you. You want to spread out and make sure there is some space between you and the people around you.

Now, I want to invite you to do a self-scan. Sit up straight with a quiet body and mouth, but please make sure you are comfortable and not too stiff. Breathe slowly and deeply here. Today, we are going to practice some gentle body movements. This means we will be slowly moving and stretching our bodies. We'll start with our feet and work our way up. As we do our gentle body movements, if you notice any other thoughts pop into your mind, just let them go without judging them. Let your thoughts float away like clouds in the sky, and then bring your attention back to your movements.

Now, focus on your toes, your feet, and your ankles. I invite you to take both of your feet and make some small, gentle circles with your ankles. Remember to keep breathing as you move. Good. Now let's do the ankle circles in the other direction. Great. Now let your toes, feet, and ankles totally relax.

Let's focus next on your legs and knees. I invite you to slowly lift one of your legs up a little bit. Move it gently and slowly in a way that feels good for you, as you breathe slowly and deeply. There is no right or wrong way to do this. Good. Now, lower that leg back down, and I invite you to slowly lift your other leg up a little bit. Move it gently and slowly, in any way that feels good for you, as you breathe. Now, bring that leg back down and feel both of your legs and knees totally relax.

Now, notice your arms, hands, and fingers. I invite you to take one hand and cross it across your chest and take the other hand and cross it over that hand to give yourself a big hug. Now, stay in that hug and lean a little bit to your right side. Take a slow, deep breath here. Now, come back to the center and pause while holding that hug. You can give yourself a little squeeze if you feel like it. Great. Now, stay in your hug and lean a little bit to your left side. Take a slow, deep breath. Now come back to the center and uncross your arms and feel your arms, hands, and fingers totally relax.

Next, we'll focus on your shoulders. I invite you to lift your shoulders up and then do some slow, gentle shoulder rolls. Good. Now do some shoulder rolls in the opposite direction. Next, bring your shoulders back down to where they belong. Pause here and breathe as you notice your shoulders totally relax.

Lastly, I welcome you to notice your neck. I invite you to slowly and gently hang your head to your right side, bringing your right ear toward your right shoulder. Relax and breathe during this side stretch. Now, come back to the center and pause. Next, you can slowly and gently hang your head to your left side, bringing your left ear toward your left shoulder. Relax and breathe during this side stretch. Come back to the center and pause here. For the last gentle movement, slowly move your chin towards your chest. Breathe and then lift your head back up.

If you feel comfortable, close your eyes. If not, gently soften them. Feel your whole body totally relaxed. Sit here for a moment in this state of total relaxation. *Pause.* Now, slowly bring your awareness back into this space and the sound of my voice. Wiggle your feet and stretch your arms as you slowly open your eyes.

Debrief:
How was that for you? Was it hard to make the slow, gentle movements? Would you like to try this next time with your eyes shut for some of the movement parts? *In a later session, you can consider inviting the children to close their eyes earlier in the script.*

Rainbow Walk (Session 5)

I want to invite you to do a self-scan. Sit up straight with a quiet body and mouth, but please make sure you are comfortable and not too stiff. Breathe in through your nose and out through your mouth. We are going to do a visualization. Remember, this means you will create a picture of something in your mind. Our visualization today is called Rainbow Walk.

Take a slow, deep breath in through your nose and a *loooong* breath out through your mouth. Again, take a slow, deep breath in through your nose and a *loooong* breath out through your mouth. If you are comfortable, you can close your eyes. If you're not comfortable, you can gently look down at your nose and soften your eyes. Listen to my voice as you breathe in through your nose and breathe out slowly and quietly through your mouth.

Imagine you are taking a walk in a field on a warm spring day. You look down at the ground and see that the colorful flowers are popping up from the dirt and beginning to bloom. As you walk toward and reach the back of the field, you notice a hill and decide to climb it. When you get to the top of the hill, you take a great big, deep breath in and out. Wow! You have never seen a sight like this before.

The most beautiful rainbow you have ever seen is right in front of you at the top of the hill. You take another breath in and step toward the rainbow. You breathe out, and, to your surprise, the bright color red surrounds your whole body, from head to toe. You feel strengthened.

You breathe in again and take another step forward, and the color orange surrounds you. You breathe out and you feel balanced. You breathe in again as you take another step forward, and the color yellow surrounds you. You breathe out and you feel hopeful.

You breathe in again as you take another step forward, and the color green surrounds you. You breathe out and feel grateful. You breathe in again as you take another step forward, and the color blue surrounds you. You breathe out and you feel peaceful.

You breathe in again as you take another step forward, and the color purple surrounds you from head to toe. You breathe out and you feel calm. You take another step forward and move out of the rainbow feeling inner strength, balance, hope, gratitude, peace, and tranquility. You walk back down the other side of the hill, and, when you get to the bottom of the hill, you sit for a moment to take everything in. *Pause.*

Now, please shift your focus back to this room and the sound of my voice. Take a deep breath in and out and think about how you feel in this moment. Slowly open your eyes.

Debrief:
How did it feel to visualize this? Were you able to see the rainbow? If not, that's okay! We'll keep practicing and get better at this. It's not easy for everyone to visualize. Did you like the exercise?

Equal Breathing (Session 6)

I want to invite you to do a self-scan. Sit up straight with a quiet body and mouth, but please make sure you are comfortable and not too stiff. Try to soften and relax your body and calm your mind as you breathe in and out, in whichever way feels comfortable for you.

In our Mindful Moment today, we will practice what's called Equal Breathing. Equal Breathing is breathing through your nose while keeping the length of your in-breath, or inhale, the same length as your out-breath, or exhale. I will count on my fingers to show you at first, and then we'll all practice together. When you are counting, you don't have to say the numbers out loud or move your fingers. You can just think of the numbers in your mind. *Demonstrate breathing in through your nose and using your fingers to count 1-2-3-4 and breathing out through your nose and using your fingers to count 1-2-3-4.*

Now, we'll try it together. As you take your next breath in through your nose, I invite you to slowly, in your mind, count to four as you breathe in. *Demonstrate counting with fingers.* And now count to four, in your mind, as you breathe out through your nose. We'll try it again. Breathe in through your nose, 1-2-3-4. Breathe out through your nose, 1-2-3-4. If you are comfortable, you can close your eyes, and we'll try equal breathing with our eyes shut. If you're not comfortable, you can gently soften your eyes and look down at your nose. Breathe in through your nose, 1-2-3-4. Breathe out through your nose, 1-2-3-4. Good. Breathe in through your nose, 1-2-3-4. Breathe out through your nose, 1-2-3-4. Breathe in through your nose, 1-2-3-4. Breathe out through your nose, 1-2-3-4. Now try equal breathing on your own for a minute. *Pause.*

I invite you to slowly bring your awareness back into this room and the sound of my voice. Think of your body sitting on the chair and your feet supporting you. Take a big breath in and hold it. Breathe out and think about how you feel right here in this space. When you are ready, please open your eyes.

Debrief:

How was Equal Breathing for you? Was it difficult? Were you able to stay focused on your counting and breaths? What did you notice? If it was tough, please remember that this is a skill that we will get better at the more we practice it.

Relaxing Happy Place (Session 7)

We will start our Mindful Moment with a self-scan. I want to invite you to notice your body, and I welcome you to sit up straight with a quiet body and mouth. Remember to please do what works best for your own body, and, as you sit up, you should feel comfortable and not too stiff. Breathe in through your nose. Breathe out and let all the tension melt out of your body.

Today, we are going to be visualizing our relaxing happy place. This can be a real place where you have been before, or it can be an imaginary place that you made up. It can even be a combination of the two. You are in control of this, and you get to decide. If you are comfortable, you can close your eyes. If you're not comfortable, you can gently soften your eyes and look down at your nose. Listen to my voice as you breathe in slowly and breathe out slowly as you relax your body and mind. I invite you to imagine that you are standing in front of an interesting staircase with five steps. Now, take a deep breath in and out, as you step onto the top stair. Notice how you feel. Continue to breathe in and out as you step down each of the steps until you reach the bottom of the stairs. *Pause.* You see a cool-looking door at the bottom of your staircase. You reach for the doorknob and open the door. You take a deep breath in and out and step inside. When you walk past the doorway, you are in your relaxing happy place. Look around. What do you see there? Are there other people around? What noises do you hear? What is the temperature? What does it feel like? Are there any smells or tastes? Are there any things to touch in your relaxing happy place? Spend a little time enjoying your special place. *Pause.*

Remember, you can close your eyes and come back to your relaxing happy place at any time. Now, I want you to slowly bring your awareness back to the sound of my voice and back to this room. Notice your body sitting on the chair and your feet supporting you. Take a big breath in and, as you breathe out, think about how you feel right now, in this very moment, after having visited your relaxing happy place. Now, stretch your body in a way that feels good for you and slowly open your eyes.

Debrief:
How was that for you? Were you able to envision your relaxing happy place? What did it look like?

Sunny Breathing Words (Session 8)

I want to invite you to do a self-scan. Sit up straight with a quiet body and mouth, but please make sure you are comfortable and not too stiff. We are going to practice breathing with Sunny Words, which means we are going to practice matching our breath to some calming words. We'll start with the words "feel peace." You will be thinking the words as I say them. You don't need to say the words aloud.

Breathe in and think of the word "feel." Now, breathe out and think of the word "peace." Breathe in and think "feel." Breathe out and think "peace." Now, if you are comfortable, let's try this with our eyes shut. If you're not comfortable, you can gently soften your eyes and look down at your nose. Breathe in and think of the word "feel." Breathe out and think of the word "peace." Breathe in "feel." Breathe out "peace." Try this on your own now. *Pause.*

Now, let's try this with the word "relax." Breathe in and think "re-." Breathe out and think "-lax." Breathe in "re-." Breathe out "-lax." Good. Now try this on your own by breathing and matching the word "relax" with the rhythm of your breath. *Pause.*

We will try one more together. We'll use the words "stay calm." Breathe in and think of the word "stay." Breathe out and think of the word "calm." Breathe in "stay." Breathe out "calm."

Good. Now try this on your own for a few cycles of breath. You might want to use your own Sunny Breathing words here. *Pause.*

Now, bring your attention back to this room and the sound of my voice. Notice your body sitting in the chair and your feet supporting you. Take a slow, deep breath in and think about how you feel right now, in this very moment. Now, stretch your arms up while you gently flutter your eyes open.

Debrief:
How did that feel that for you? Were you able to pair your words with your breath? Did you use your own Sunny Breathing word?

Positive Self-Talk (Session 9)

I want to invite you to do a self-scan. Sit up straight with a quiet body and mouth, but please make sure you are comfortable and not too stiff. Breathe in and, as you breathe out, try to relax your body. Today's Mindful Moment is about positive self-talk, which are helpful, happy words you can say to yourself.

Take a couple of cycles of slow, deep breaths, and, if you are comfortable, close your eyes. If you're not comfortable, you can gently soften your gaze and look down at your nose.

Allow yourself to become as relaxed as you can. Take some slow, deep breaths as you listen to the words. You can repeat the words in your mind after I say them if you want, but you don't need to say the words out loud. Just think the words in your head.

I am relaxed. *Pause.*
I am calm. *Pause.*
I accept my feelings. *Pause.*
I can handle hard things. *Pause.*
I appreciate myself. *Pause.*
I feel peaceful. *Pause.*

Now, I want you to slowly bring your awareness back into this room and the sound of my voice. Take a deep breath in and out and think about how you feel right now. Slowly open your eyes and come back to the present.

Debrief:
How was that for you? How did it feel? Were there certain self-talk phrases that you really liked? Are there other helpful, happy words or phrases you would like to add?

Hot Air Balloon Ride (Session 10)

I want to invite you to do a self-scan. Sit up straight with a quiet body and mouth and, please, make sure you are comfortable. We are going to do a visualization. Remember, this means you create a picture of something in your mind. Our visualization today is called Hot Air Balloon Ride.

Breathe in and out in any way that feels good to you. If you are comfortable, you can close your eyes. If you're not comfortable, you can gently soften your eyes and look down at your nose. Listen to my voice as you breathe in slowly through your nose and breathe out slowly and quietly through your mouth.

Imagine you won a ticket to take a special hot air balloon ride. The ride will fit as many people as you need it to, so you can take all of the people who support you — the people who help you when you have big feelings and the people who really look out for you. Your supportive people could be your family, friends, teachers, counselors, coaches, neighbors, or anyone else you know that supports you. You might even choose to have special pets with you on your hot air balloon ride. You step onto the hot air balloon first and stand in the middle, and then each of your supportive people steps on behind you. Your heart fills with happiness, being surrounded by all these people who care about you. The driver of the hot air balloon asks you where you want to fly to. They can take you to any place you want to go. You tell the driver where you want to go, and the hot air balloon lifts off. All your supportive people cheer as the hot air balloon rises into the clouds. It is so beautiful floating in the sky! You see all kinds of cool things below as your hot air balloon flies around. Take a minute to imagine all the beautiful things you can see. *Pause.* You feel amazing after your ride, and now it's time for your hot air balloon to land. You and all your supportive people each take turns stepping off. Now, I want you to bring your attention back to this space, and I ask you to slowly think about this room and the sound of my voice. Take a deep breath in and out and think about how you feel in this moment. Slowly open your eyes and come back to the present.

Debrief:
How was that for you? How did you feel to be surrounded by your supportive people? Who were your supports? What cool things did you see from the hot air balloon ride?

Present Moment (Session 11)

I want to invite you to do a self-scan. Sit up straight, but comfortably, with a quiet body and mouth. We are going to practice mindfulness and gratitude today.

Mindfulness means paying attention to the present moment. A great way to be mindful is to tune into your breath. If you are comfortable, I welcome you to close your eyes, or you can gently soften your eyes and look down at your nose.

Try to notice your breath. If any thoughts pop into your head, just let them go and bring your focus back on your breath. Feel the movement of your breath as it comes in and leaves your body. In and out. *Pause.*

Now, think of something you are grateful for. It might be a person, a place, an animal, a type of food, a toy, or something else. Let that thankfulness fill you up, and hold onto that warm, happy feeling inside of you as you breathe in and out. *Pause.*

Tune into your breath and let any other thoughts that come up float away. *Pause*

Now, please shift your focus and think of yourself sitting in this room. Take a deep breath in and out and think about how you feel right now. Slowly open your eyes as you stretch in whichever way feels good for you as you come back to the present moment.

Debrief:
How was that for you? Were you able to stay mindful in the present moment? What did you notice? Were you able to think of something you are grateful for?

Bridge (Session 12)

I want to invite you to do a self-scan. Sit up straight, but comfortably, with a quiet body and mouth. We are going to do a visualization called Bridge.

Breathe in and out, in any way that feels good to you. If you are comfortable, you can close your eyes or gently soften your gaze and look down at your nose. Listen to my voice as you breathe in and out slowly and deeply. If any thoughts come up, just allow them to pass and bring your attention back to your breath or my voice. I'll be asking some questions during the visualization. Remember to think of the answers in your head; you don't have to say them out loud.

Imagine you are walking in an interesting place and you see a very cool-looking bridge up ahead. You decide to walk onto it. Each time you take a step on the bridge, you breathe in and out. In and out. *Pause.* When you are about halfway through the bridge, you look behind you. What do you see behind you? *Pause.* Then, you look in front of you. What do you see up ahead? *Pause.*

You keep walking and moving forward. Before you reach the bridge's end, you take a big, deep breath in and then breathe out slow. You step off the bridge, feeling refreshed, calm, and relaxed.

Now, I want you to bring your attention back into this room. Think about this space and your body sitting in the chair. Take a deep breath in and out and think about how you feel right now. Slowly open your eyes and stretch your body in whichever way feels good for you, as you come back to the present moment.

Debrief:
What was your experience like? Were you able to visualize the bridge and what was behind you and in front of you?

Our Group Agreements

Our Plan for Today

Our Group Agreements

Mindful Moment

Feelings Check

Workbook Activities

Mindful Moment

Feelings Check

The Triangle

Thoughts

Behavior

Feelings

Feelings Brainstorm List

_____   _____

_____   _____

_____   _____

_____   _____

_____   _____

_____   _____

Self-Scan

Look down at your self.

Scan your body to see if it is doing what is expected.
Where are your arms and hands? Where should they be? Are you touching things?

Where are your legs and feet? Where should they be?

How close are you to other people?

Adjust as needed.

Measuring Challenges

Huge Volcano

Big Hill

Medium Boulder

Small Rock

Data Collection Sheet

Skill:		Date:

Name:	Data:	# correct out of the total #

Key:

✔ = correct independently

? = did not answer

<u>✔</u> = correct with assistance

✘ = incorrect

Skills for Big Feelings Survey

1.   If I have big feelings, I know what to do.   *yes / kind of / no*

2.   I know how to measure challenges.   *yes / kind of / no*

3.   I have been using the skills I learned.   *yes / kind of / no*

4.   I feel _____ about being in group.

5.   Three favorite skills I learned are: _____

_____

_____

_____

6.   My supports are: _____

_____

7.   What does F-B-T-S stand for?

        F = _____   B = _____

        T = _____   S = _____

On the back, please write anything else you would like to share with me.

Skills for Big Feelings Parent/Guardian Survey

Please fill out the survey below and return it to me by _____ . I appreciate your help!

	Strongly Disagree	Disagree	Undecided	Agree	Strongly Agree
As a whole, my child appeared to enjoy the Skills for Big Feelings program.	1	2	3	4	5
I believe my child has made positive changes by being involved in this program.	1	2	3	4	5
My child is able to tell me what they have learned in the Skills for Big Feelings program.	1	2	3	4	5
My child is practicing the skills they learned.	1	2	3	4	5
My child appeared to have a positive relationship with the facilitator.	1	2	3	4	5

Please describe any changes you have seen in your child and share anything else you would like to add:

MY SKILLS FOR BIG FEELINGS WORKBOOK

By: _____

Feeling-Breath-Thought-Skill

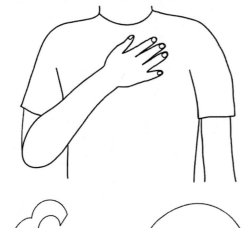

Name your
FEELINGS

Take 3 slow,
deep **BREATHS**

Choose helpful,
happy **THOUGHTS**

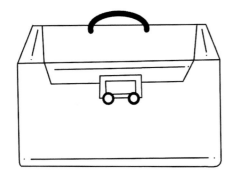

Pick a **SKILL**
to practice

What My Big Feelings Look and Feel Like

Flying Bird

Cross your arms on your chest with your fingers pointed up towards your neck. Interlock your thumbs. Take some slow, deep belly breaths while you tap your hands, or wings, in a pattern — one and then the other.

Smell the Flower

Imagine you are holding a flower and breathe in through your nose to smell the wonderful scent. Next, pretend you are blowing out a candle by blowing air out through tight lips.

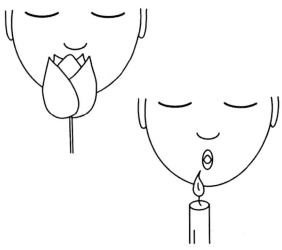

Frog Mouth

Pretend you are a frog and open your mouth as wide as you can to stretch your jaw wide open. Hold the stretch for ten seconds. Now relax and release your mouth as much as you can and use your hands to massage your jaw on both sides. Do you feel the difference between the tense and the loose sensations?

My Triggers

- *Circle your triggers, or the things that bother you A LOT.*
- *Cross out the things that don't bother you too much.*
- *Check your top 3 triggers.*

1. When things change
2. When things are too loud
3. Feeling tired
4. Using too much technology
5. Being told no
6. Being in a big crowd
7. When someone is being rude
8. When things are messy
9. Being hungry
10. Not moving around enough

11. When there is bad weather
12. Having too much to do
13. Not knowing what will happen
14. Being the center of attention
15. Being bored
16. When someone is being teased
17. Not being able to finish something
18. Changing from one thing to another

Do you have other triggers that aren't listed?

Sun and Sand

Envision you are at the beach on a beautiful summer day. Sit criss-cross applesauce on the sand. Breathe in and stretch your arms up high above your head, reaching towards the sun and lengthening your body. Feel your shoulders stretch. Now, breathe out and reach your arms out in front of you towards the sand. Hold the stretch for ten seconds and relax here.

Gorilla Hug

Wrap your arms around your torso and give yourself a big, giant gorilla hug. Squeeze if it feels comfortable. Uncross your arms and try again with the opposite arm on top. Uncross your arms and now try giving yourself a big, giant gorilla hug over your shoulders. Now try again with the opposite arm on top.

Snowman Stress Melter Breath

Place your pointer finger on the bow tie and follow the arrows as you trace your finger around the snowman's head while you breathe in. When you come back to the bow tie, start to breathe out a very long and slow breath as you trace your finger around the snowman's body. Repeat and feel your stress melt away.

Helpful and Unhelpful Thoughts

Circle the helpful thoughts that would make someone feel good.
Cross out the unhelpful thoughts that would make someone feel lousy.

1. I can handle this.

2. She is so much better at reading than I am.

3. This is way too hard for me.

4. I'm feeling mad. It'll be okay. This feeling will go away.

5. This isn't fair.

6. This is just a feeling. I will be okay.

7. I will never get all this work done.

8. I can do hard things.

9. It's okay if I can't finish now. I'll do it later.

Snail Shell

Imagine you are a snail in a lovely garden with beautiful flowers all around. Take a break from the garden by hiding inside your snail shell. Gently push your head down to hide inside your shell as you lift your shoulders up towards your head. Hold this position for ten seconds. Now, take a big breath in and stretch out of your shell by lifting your head and heart up high and pulling your shoulders back down as you breathe out.

Flat Tire

Breathe in while flexing your arms up above your head to make a tire shape. Now, breathe out while very gently and slowly lowering your arms and making a "shhh" sound. All of the air drains out of the tire just as all of the stress flows out of your body.

Helpful, Happy Thoughts

When you think helpful, happy thoughts, you will feel good. When you think unhelpful thoughts, you won't feel good. What do you like to think about? Think about helpful, happy things that you like, whether they're memories, games, animals, places, music, or people. If you are comfortable, close your eyes for a minute and think of your helpful, happy thoughts.

My Helpful, Happy Thoughts

Thought Changer

Change the unhelpful thoughts into more helpful thoughts.

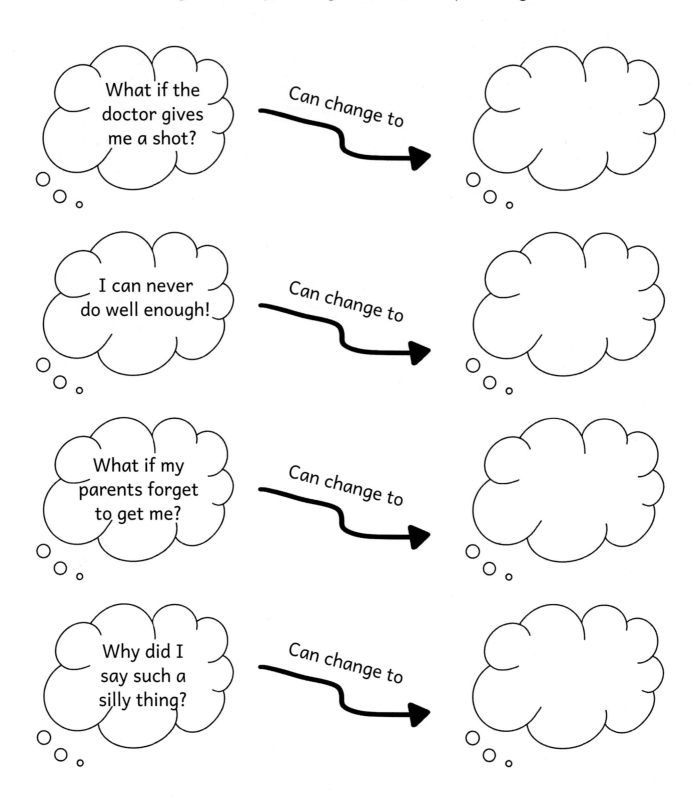

Fly Away, Ladybug

Imagine a lucky ladybug landed on your nose and is tickling you. You don't want to use your hands to touch her, but you want her to fly away home. So, pucker up your face really tight. Squeeze your nose and eyes. Feel all the wrinkles and stiffness in your forehead, cheeks, mouth, and eyes. Hold this position for ten seconds. Now, relax and loosen all of your face muscles so they melt into softness again.

Buddy Breath

Lie down and place an object, such as a stuffed animal, on your belly. Take a slow, deep breath in, filling your belly up with air, and watch your object lift up and rise. Now, breathe out very slowly and watch your object slowly fall. Repeat with slow, deep breaths in and out, as you watch your object rise and fall gently with the rhythm of your breath.

Elephant Ears

Take your thumbs and pointer fingers, and place them on your ear lobes. Pull down gently and lightly massage, starting at the bottom of your ear lobe and working your way up to the top of your ear.

Measuring Challenges

For each challenge, write down whether it is a small rock,
medium boulder, big hill, or huge volcano challenge.

1. You are choking.   _____

2. A bully threatens you and pushes you down.   _____

3. You have a headache.   _____

4. Someone you love is very sick in the hospital.   _____

5. You can't have extra dessert.   _____

6. You raise your hand but didn't get called on.   _____

7. Your friend sits with someone else on the bus.   _____

8. You drop your pencil.   _____

9. You have a substitute teacher.   _____

10. There is a fire.   _____

11. You and your friend got into an argument.   _____

12. Someone cuts you in line.   _____

13. You lose in a game.   _____

Huge Volcano

 Big Hill

 Medium Boulder

 Small Rock

Measuring Challenges

If you have a challenge, take three deep breaths, then ask yourself how big the challenge is. Is your response equal to the challenge? If not, which skills will you use choose to cool down?

Ski Jumper

Raise both of your arms up above your head and then swing them back behind you, as you bend slightly forward at the waist while keeping your back straight. Now continue to swing your arms, as you rock forward and backward and feel the air rushing by your arms. When you lean forward, your arms swing back, and, when you lean back, your arms swing forward.

Balloon Breath

Interlace your fingers and place them on your belly. Imagine you are using your breath to inflate a balloon in front of your belly. What color is your balloon? Breathe in and slowly lift your arms out in front of you as the balloon blows up. Now, breathe out through your mouth to make a "pfft" raspberry blowing sound with your lips as you slowly lower your arms back down, making the balloon deflate.

Equal Measurements

Circle the scenarios in which the reaction is equal to the challenge.

Cross out the scenarios in which the reaction does not match the challenge.

Huge
Volcano

Big Hill

Medium
Boulder

Small
Rock

1. Your pencil breaks and you cry for an hour.

2. You can't go to the movies, so you throw markers.

3. Someone cuts you in line and you shrug it off.

4. Someone is taking too long at the water fountain, so you yell at them.

5. You make a mistake and rip up your paper.

6. Someone pokes you and you ask them to stop.

7. You have a substitute teacher and tell yourself, "I can handle this."

8. You drop your ice cream on the floor and politely ask if you can have another one.

9. Someone bumps into you by accident and you scream.

Orange Squeeze

Imagine you are holding oranges in both of your hands and squeeze the oranges as tight as you can to make orange juice. Hold the squeeze for ten seconds and squeeze every last drop out. Now relax your hands. Can you feel the difference between feeling tense and feeling relaxed? Now, breathe in and squeeze the oranges, and then breathe out and let the oranges drop.

Equal Breathing

Breathe in through your nose while counting to four in your head. Breathe out through your nose while counting to four in your head. You want to match the size of your inhale to the size of your exhale as you take slow, deep breaths through your nose.

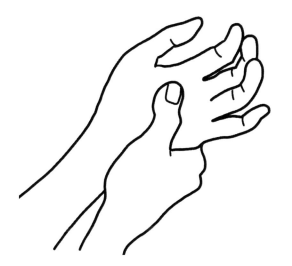

Hand Massage

Hold your left hand in your right and put your right thumb on the pad of your left palm under your pointer finger. Use your thumb to massage in circles, working your way from the inside to the outside of your palm. Next, squeeze and pinch each fingertip. Now, flip your hand and rub the top of it. Repeat on the other hand.

My Relaxing Happy Place

Imagine Your Relaxing Happy Place

If you are comfortable, close your eyes and take three slow, deep breaths . . . Now, imagine your relaxing happy place. Look around. What do you see there? Are there other people around? What noises do you hear? What is the temperature? What does it feel like? Are there any smells or tastes?

Bumble Bee Breath

With your lips sealed firmly, take a deep breath in through your nose. Now breathe out and make an "mmm" sound, like a bumble bee buzzing. Try to make your exhale buzz as long as you can. If you are comfortable, you can try it again while covering your ears.

Door Squeeze

Imagine you are playing hide-and-go-seek with your friends, and you want to sneak through a door quietly. Sit or stand up very tall and straight, and suck your stomach in. Now, hold your stomach tightly for ten seconds to make it through the door. Remember to continue to breathe as you hold your stomach muscles tightly! Okay, now relax and unclench your stomach.

Unicorn Breath

Place your pointer finger on the sparkle. Trace the unicorn horn down the right side as you breathe in through your nose. Next, trace the bottom of the unicorn horn from right to left as you hold your breath in. Finally, trace the unicorn horn up from the bottom to top as you breathe out. Repeat and feel the unicorn sparkle!

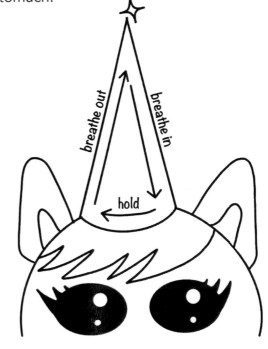

My Sunny Breathing Words

Circle all of the words you would like to try Sunny Breathing with. Write the word or words you like the most inside the sun. Make up your own Sunny Breathing words to try!

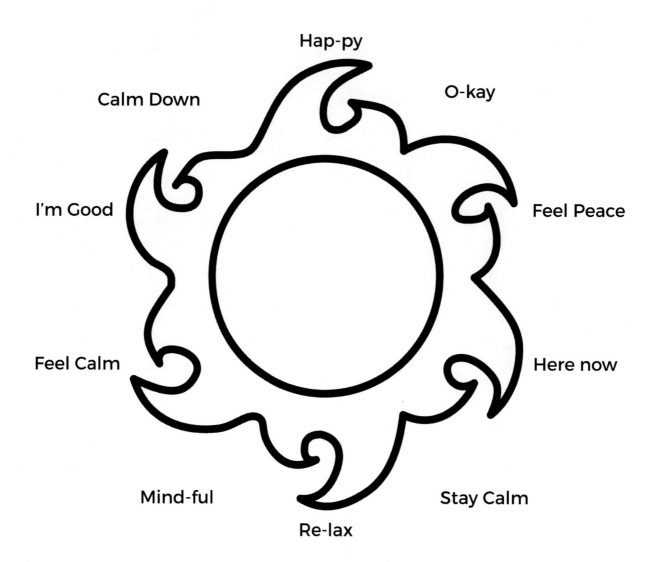

Hap-py

O-kay

Calm Down

Feel Peace

I'm Good

Feel Calm

Here now

Mind-ful

Stay Calm

Re-lax

Ice Cream Twist

Stand up and cross one ankle over the other. Put your arms out straight in front of you, and then turn your thumbs towards the floor so your palms are facing out. Cross one wrist over the other and interlace your fingers together. Then turn your hands in towards your heart. Breathe in and out through your nose slowly as you place your tongue on the top of your mouth. Untwist yourself and try crossing your ankles and wrists in the opposite direction.

Finger Aerobics

Start with an open hand. Breathe in and out through your nose while touching your thumb to pinky. Breathe in and out through your nose while touching your thumb to your ring finger. Breathe in and out through your nose while touching your thumb to your middle finger. Breathe in and out through your nose while touching your thumb to your pointer finger. Switch hands and try it again. Then, try it with both hands at the same time.

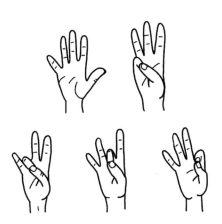

Counting for Calm

Count ten slow, deep breaths while you think about each number. Then count backward from ten to one while breathing slowly and deeply. You can also try skip-counting while breathing if you want to experiment. Repeat until you feel calm.

Positive Self-Talk

Circle the positive self-talk examples that you think will be the most helpful for you. Write down your own positive self-talk in the empty bubbles!

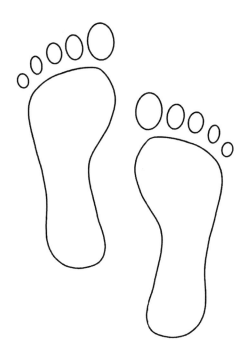

Sandy Toes

Imagine you are barefoot at a beautiful beach, standing in the sand near the shoreline. Bend your knees to press your legs and feet as far down into the sand as you can. Curl and press your toes down into the floor and hold for ten seconds. Now, shake your feet and legs out and feel them loosen and relax.

High-Five Breath

Open your hand up like you are going to give a high-five. Take your other pointer finger and place it at the base of your thumb. Slide up your thumb slowly as you breathe in, and slide down your thumb slowly as you breathe out. Repeat this movement and breathing for each finger. Then, trace the other hand.

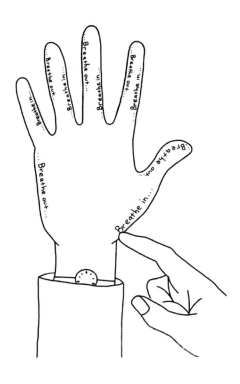

Strong Tree Blowing

It is a very windy day, and you are a strong tree that is slowly blowing back and forth in the wind. Reach your arms up above your head as you breathe in. Interlace your fingers above your head. Bend at the waist to your left as you breathe out. Breathe in and come back to the center. Now, breathe out and bend at the waist to your right. Breathe in and come back to the center. Lower your arms down slowly by your side.

My Supports

Tap Tap Squeeze

Tap your right hand to your left shoulder and think of the word "I." Tap your left hand to your right shoulder and think of the word "am." Then, squeeze both hands together and think of the word "calm." Repeat the "tap tap squeeze" motion while thinking the phrase "I am calm" with each movement.

Flip Flop Nostril Breath

Press your right thumb against your right nostril and breathe in slowly and deeply through your open left nostril. Then, lift your thumb up and place your pointer finger on the left nostril and breathe out and then breathe in through the right open nostril. Then, lift your pointer finger up and press your right thumb against your right nostril again, breathing out and in slowly and deeply through your open left nostril. Repeat in this pattern.

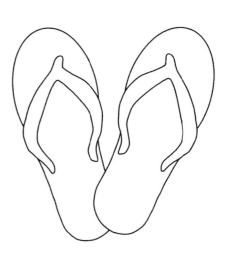

Letting Go

If you are comfortable, close your eyes, and visualize you are holding a balloon. Imagine blowing all of your big feelings into the balloon, tying the balloon, letting it go, and watching it float away into the sky. As the balloon floats away and disappears, you feel calmer and more peaceful.

Mindfulness and Gratitude

*Being **mindful** means paying attention, on purpose, to what is happening right now, in the present moment. When you are being mindful, you aren't judging what is happening; you are just observing it.*

*Being **grateful**, or having gratitude, means that you realize what you are thankful for. Being mindful, or paying attention on purpose, helps you be more grateful. When you are grateful, it's a happy, helpful thought, so you feel good.*

Things I am Grateful For:

A person I am grateful for: _____

A food I am grateful for: _____

A thing I am grateful for: _____

A place I am grateful for: _____

A show I am grateful for: _____

A memory I am grateful for: _____

Shake Wiggle Shake

Put on some music and begin by shaking and wiggling one foot. Then, shake and wiggle the other foot. Then, shake and wiggle each leg. Then, shake and wiggle your hips. Then, shake and wiggle your hands, arms, and shoulders. Then, shake and wiggle your neck and head. Now your whole body is shaking and wiggling!

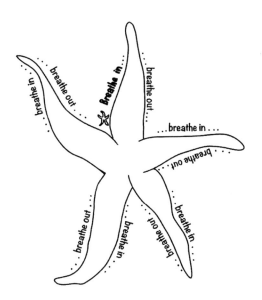

Starfish Breath

Place your pointer finger on the baby starfish. Trace up as you breathe in, and trace down as you breathe out. Trace the pattern, breathing in and breathing out, as each arm of the starfish is traced, and you feel relaxed and calm.

Steel to Jelly

Breathe in and tense all the muscles in your whole body as if they are made of steel. Tense your feet, legs, stomach, arms, hands, shoulders, neck, face, and jaw. As you slowly breathe out, relax and loosen all of your body's muscles as if they are turning from steel to jelly. Relax your feet, legs, stomach, arms, hands, shoulders, neck, and face.

In the Driver's Seat

Circle the things you can control. Cross out the things that you cannot control.

1. The weather

2. Someone else is yelling

3. Other people's choices

4. Your friends

5. Your actions

6. Your thoughts

7. Your attitude

8. How often you smile

9. Someone saying something rude

10. Your feelings

11. Your ideas

12. Your effort

13. Other people's effort

14. Your words

15. Your choices

16. Being kind

17. Your family

18. Someone else's thoughts

More things I can control:

Finger Lock

Lift your right arm straight up at heart level, and then bend it towards you. Point your right thumb down and curl your fingers in. Take your left arm and curl your left fingers underneath your right fingers. Breathe in as you pull your fingers against each other. Breathe out as you relax, soften, and release.

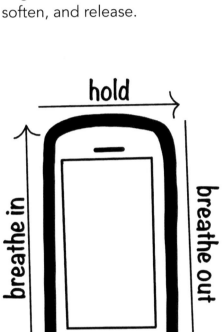

Cell Phone Breath

Start by placing your pointer finger on the star. Breathe in as you trace the cell phone up along the left side. Hold your breath in as you trace the top of the phone. Breathe out as you trace the right side of the phone. Now, hold your breath out as you trace along the bottom of the phone. Repeat.

Grounding

Look around you. Take a slow, deep breath. Use your senses to name five things you can see. Name four things you can touch. Name three things you can hear. Name two things you can smell, and name one thing you can taste.

5, 4, 3, 2, 1

My Top Five Favorite Skills

THANK YOU AND ACKNOWLEDGMENTS

What Did You Think of Skills for Big Feelings?

First of all, thank you for purchasing *Skills for Big Feelings*! I know you could have picked any number of books, but you picked this book, and, for that, I am extremely grateful.

I hope you found this book useful and your children enjoyed the activities. If you do find this book helpful, it would be wonderful if you could tell your friends and colleagues about it or share your thoughts on social media. I'd also love to hear from you and hope that you could take some time to post a review online. Your feedback and support will help with future projects and enable me to make this book even better.

Please follow me on social media and go to my website at http://www.wholechildcounseling.com to join my mailing list. By joining my mailing list, you'll have access to my free resource library, and I will continue to add supplemental learning and activities there related to *Skills for Big Feelings.*

Acknowledgements

I want to express gratitude to my sister Billie, who always encourages my creativity, and to my husband, Aaron, for always being supportive of all my ideas and projects. I also want to thank my children, Simon and Oliver and all of my beta testers for their feedback.

ABOUT THE AUTHOR

Casey O'Brien Martin is a passionate individual who aspires to bring out the best in each person she works with. She has a Master of Arts in expressive arts therapy and mental health counseling from Lesley University. She is a licensed School Adjustment Counselor, a Registered Expressive Arts Therapist, a Licensed Mental Health Counselor, and a Registered Nurse. She has experience working with diverse populations in schools, hospitals, group homes, community centers, and outpatient treatment environments. She currently serves as an Adjunct Faculty Member in the Graduate School of Arts and Social Sciences at Lesley University.

Casey considers working with children each day a privilege. Her specialization includes using the arts and a holistic approach to help each child grow as a confident and independent person. She has a longstanding interest in mind/body medicine. She combines her unique background in expressive arts therapy, nursing, and mental health counseling, with herbalism studies to craft comprehensive mind-body focused programs to help each child achieve their highest potential. For more information, please visit http://www.wholechildcounseling.com.

REFERENCES

American Academy of Pediatrics (2009). From the American academy of pediatrics: policy statement-media violence. *Pediatrics, 124*(5), 1495-1503. https://doi.org/10.1542/peds.2009-2146

American Academy of Pediatrics (2014, June 7). *Brush, book, bed: how to structure your child's nighttime routine.* Healthy Children. http://bit.ly/bedroutine

American Academy of Pediatrics (2016, June 13). *American academy of pediatrics supports childhood sleep guidelines.* American Academy of Pediatrics. https://www.healthychildren.org/English/news/Pages/AAP-Supports-Childhood-Sleep-Guidelines.aspx

American Academy of Pediatrics (2016, October 21). *American academy of pediatrics announces new recommendations for children's media use.* Healthy Children. https://www.healthychildren.org/English/news/Pages/AAP-Announces-New-Recommendations-for-Childrens-Media-Use.aspx

American School Counselors Association (2014). *ASCA mindsets and behaviors for student success: K-12 college- and career-readiness standards for every student.* American School Counselor Association. https://www.schoolcounselor.org/asca/media/asca/home/MindsetsBehaviors.pdf

American School Counselor Association. (n.d.) *School Counseling Data Specialist.* American School Counselor Association. https://www.schoolcounselor.org/school-counselors/professional-development/asca-u-specialist-trainings/school-counseling-data-specialist

Applestein, C. D. (1998). *No such thing as a bad kid! Understanding and responding to the challenging behavior of troubled children and youth.* Gifford School.

Bjerke, M. B., and Renger, R. (2017). Being smart about writing SMART objectives. *Evaluation and Program Planning, 61,* 125–127. http://doi:10.1016/j.evalprogplan.2016.12.009

Borysenko, J. (1988). *Minding the body, mending the mind.* Bantam Books.

Brown, B. (2019, August 7). *What Toni Morrison taught me about parenting.* Brené Brown. https://brenebrown.com/blog/2019/08/07/what-toni-morrison-taught-me-about-parenting/

Centers for Disease Control and Prevention. (2019, April 19). *Data and statistics on children's mental health.* Centers for Disease Control and Prevention. https://www.cdc.gov/childrenmentalhealth/data.html

Center on the Developing Child. (2015). *The science of resilience (in brief).* Center on the Developing Child Harvard University. https://developingchild.harvard.edu/resources/inbrief-the-science-of-resilience/

Chaddock-Heyman, L., Hillman, C. H., Cohen, N. J. & Kramer, A. F. (2014). The importance of physical activity and aerobic fitness for cognitive control and memory in children. *Monographs of the Society for Research in Child Development, 79*(14), 25-50. https://doi.org/10.1111/mono.12129

Chandler, P. & Tricot, A. (2015). Mind your body: the essential role of body movements in children's learning. *Educational Psychology Review, 27*(3), 365-370. http://doi.org/10.1007/s10648-015-9333-3

CHOC Children's. (n.d.) *Guided Imagery.* CHOC Children's. https://www.choc.org/programs-services/integrative-health/guided-imagery/

Collaborative for Academic, Social, and Emotional Learning (CASEL). (2019). *Core SEL competencies.* Collaborative for Academic, Social, and Emotional Learning (CASEL). https://casel.org/core-competencies/

Eaton, J. and Tieber, C. (2017). The effects of coloring on anxiety, mood, and perseverance. *Journal of the American Art Therapy Association, 34*(1), 42-46. https://doi.org/10.1080/07421656.2016.1277113

Evans, R. (1971). *Richard Evans' quote book.* Publishers Press.

Ginott, H. G. (1972). *Between teacher and child.* Scribner Book Company.

Greene, R. W. (2009). *Kids do well if they can.* Lives in the Balance. https://www.livesinthebalance.org/kids-do-well-if-they-can

Greene. R. W. (2020). *Compassionate communities.* Lives in the Balance. https://www.livesinthebalance.org/compassionate-community

Hadlington, L., White, H. and Curtis, S. (2019). "I cannot live without my [tablet]": Children's experiences of using tablet technology within the home. *Computers in Human Behavior, 94,* 19-24. https://doi.org/10.1016/j.chb.2018.12.043

Hinz, L. D. (2020). *Expressive therapies continuum: A framework for using art in therapy.* Routledge.

Ichiki, Y. and Hinz, L. D. (2015). *Exploring media properties and the expressive therapies continuum: Survey of art therapists.* Paper presented at the 46th Annual American Art Therapy Association conference, Minneapolis, MN.

Jordan, J. V. (2010) *Relational-Cultural Therapy.* American Psychological Association.

Jung, C. (n.d.), as cited in Seltzer, L. F. (2016, June 15). You only get more of what you resist-why? *Psychology Today.* https://www.psychologytoday.com/us/blog/evolution-the-self/201606/you-only-get-more-what-you-resist-why

Kearney, D. J. and Simpson, T. L. (2020). *Mindfulness-based interventions for trauma and its consequences.* American Psychological Association.

Kendall, P. C., Swan, A. J., Carper, M. M., & Hoff, A. L. (2018). Anxiety disorders among children and adolescents. In J. N. Butcher & P. C. Kendall (Eds.), *APA handbooks in psychology®. APA handbook of psychopathology: Child and adolescent psychopathology* (pp. 213–230). American Psychological Association.

Kessler, R. C., Berglund, P., Demler, O., Jin, R., Merikangas, K. R., & Walters, E. E. (2005). Lifetime prevalence and age-of-onset distributions of DSM-IV disorders in the National Comorbidity Survey Replication. *Archives of General Psychiatry, 62*(6), 593–602. https://www.doi.org/10.1001/archpsyc.62.6.593

Kohn, A. (1999). *Punished by rewards: The trouble with gold stars, incentive plans, A's, praise and other bribes.* Mariner Books.

Media Education Foundation. (n.d.) *Media violence: facts and statistics.* https://www.mediaed.org/handouts/ChildrenMedia.pdf

McMahon, E. M., Corcoran, P., O'Regan, G., Keeley, H., Cannon, M., Carli, V., Wasserman, C., Hadlaczky, G., Sarchiapone, M., Apter, A., Balazs, J., Balint, M., Bobes, J., Brunner, R., Cozman, D., Haring, C., Iosue, M., Kaess, M., Kahn, J., ... Wasserman, D. (2017). Physical activity in European adolescents and associations with anxiety, depression and well-being. *European Child and Adolescent Psychiatry, (1)*111. https://www.doi.org/10.1007/s00787-016-0875-9

Miguel Ruiz, D. (1999). *The Four Agreements: A practical guide to personal freedom.* Amber-Allen Publishing.

Minahan, J. (2014). *The behavior code companion: Strategies, tools, and interventions for supporting children with anxiety-related or oppositional behaviors.* Harvard Education Press.

Minahan, J. and Rappaport, N. (2012). *The behavior code: A practical guide to understanding and teaching the most challenging children.* Harvard Education Press.

O'Neil, A., Quirk, S. E, Housden, S., Brennan, S. L, Williams, L. J, Pasco, J. A, Berk, M. & Jacka, F. N. (2014). Relationship between diet and mental health in children and adolescents: a systematic review. *American Journal of Public Health, (104)*10, e31-e42. https://www.doi.org/10.2105/AJPH.2014.302110

Paruthi, S., Brooks, L. J., D'Ambrosio, C., Hall, W. A., Kotagal, S., Lloyd, R. M., Malow, B. A., Maski, K., Nichols, C., Quan, S. F., Rosen, C. L., Troester, M. M., & Wise, M. S. (2016). Recommended amount of sleep for pediatric populations: A consensus statement of the American Academy of Sleep Medicine. *Journal of clinical sleep medicine: official publication of the American Academy of Sleep Medicine, 12*(6), 785–786. https://www.doi.org/10.5664/jcsm.5866

Platt, R., Williams, S. R. and Ginsburg, G. S. (2016). Stressful life events and child anxiety: Examining parent and child mediators. *Child Psychiatry and Human Development, 47*(1), 23-34. https://www.doi.org/10.1007/s10578-015-0540-4

Regev, D. and Snir, S. (2018). *Parent-child art psychotherapy.* Routledge/Taylor and Francis Group.

Rose, C. (Executive Producer). (2003, February 27). Remembering Fred Rogers (Season 2, Episode 19). [TV series episode]. In C. Rose (Executive Producer), *The Charlie Rose Show.* Public Broadcasting System.

Siegel, D. J., and Payne Bryson, T. (2011). *The whole-brain child: 12 revolutionary strategies to nurture your child's developing mind.* Random House.

Siddiqi, A. [@AyeshaASiddiqi]. (2013, May 15). *Be person you needed when you were younger* [Tweet]. Twitter. https://twitter.com/ayeshaasiddiqi/status/334747947222855680?lang=en

Spence, S. H. (1994). *Spence Children's Anxiety Scale*. Spence Children's Anxiety Scale Website. https://www.scaswebsite.com/

Thomas, M. L. (2006). The contributing factors of change in a therapeutic process. *Contemporary Family Therapy, 28*, 201-210. https://www.doi.org/10.1007/s10591-006-9000-4

Treleaven, D. A. (2018). *Trauma-sensitive mindfulness: Practices for safe and transformative healing*. New York: W.W Norton & Company.

Young, A. and Kaffenberger, C. (2018). *Making data work: An ASCA national model publication*. Perfect Paperback.

Zhu, X., Heagele, J. A. & Healy, S. (2019) Movement and mental health: behavioral correlates of anxiety and depression among children of 6-17 years old in the U.S. *Mental Health and Physical Activity 16*, 60-65. https://doi.org/10.1016/j.mhpa.2019.04.002

Made in United States
North Haven, CT
13 September 2024

57334776R00100